Contents

Editors' Foreword

The series of which this book is a part is designed to meet the needs of students in Sixth Forms and those taking courses in further and higher education. In assessing these needs two factors especially have been taken into account: the limits on the student's time which preclude the reading of all the important scholarly works, and the importance of providing stimulus to thought and imagination. Therefore the series, which has considerably more space available than even the larger single-volume textbooks on the period, presents the interpretations which have altered or increased our understanding of the age, as well as including sufficient detail to illustrate and enliven the subject. Most important of all, emphasis has been placed on discussion. Instead of outlining supposedly established facts, problems are posed as they were faced by the people of the time and as they confront the historian today in his task of interpretation. The student is thus enabled to approach the subject in an attitude of enquiry, and is encouraged to exercise his own mind on the arguments, never closed, of historiography. In so doing he will gain some knowledge of the methods of historians and of the kinds of evidence they use. He should also find enjoyment by the way.

The arrangement of the series, with several volumes covering particular aspects over a long period, and others with more strict chronological limits, has enabled each author to concentrate on an area of special interest, and should make for flexibility in use by the reader.

K.H.R.
J.W.H.

Full details of historical works referred to in the text will be found in the list of Further Reading on page 125. Only where the work is not included is a full reference given in the text.

Chapter I

'A free hand'

1 **Lord Salisbury and the fundamentals of British foreign policy** Robert Arthur Talbot Cecil (1830–1903) succeeded his brother as Viscount Cranborne in 1865 and his father as 3rd Marquis of Salisbury in 1868. He was Foreign Secretary 1878–80, 1885–6, 1887–92 and 1895–1900; and Prime Minister June 1885 to February 1886, August 1886 to 1892 and 1895–1902: very nearly as long as Palmerston as Foreign Secretary and longer than anyone else as Prime Minister since the Reform Act of 1832. He was the last Prime Minister in the House of Lords. He himself was much surprised to find himself Prime Minister, for when he succeeded his father in 1868 he had supposed this put paid to his becoming leader of the Conservative Party. But the ineffectiveness of Sir Stafford Northcote, leader in the House of Commons on Disraeli's elevation to the peerage in 1876, and the unexpected gift for popular leadership that Salisbury revealed during Gladstone's second ministry ensured his choice as leader of the party, and so in due course as Prime Minister.

Being in the Lords removed him from the hurly-burly of the House of Commons and automatically made him more aloof from the rank and file and from his colleagues. This aloofness was increased by his rank, his temperament and his method of working. He was a direct descendant of the Elizabethan Lord Burghley and so belonged to one of the great aristocratic English families. He was an intellectual, a shy man very reserved outside his own family, with no taste for society, no small talk and no

9

memory for faces. It is recorded that once he asked his host at a breakfast party who the stranger was sitting on his left, only to be told that it was his old colleague W. H. Smith, at that moment the second man in his Cabinet.

He was a Christian sceptic. The fundamentals of his faith were so firm and so unshaken by his unhappy childhood and adolescence and by mid-Victorian rationalistic 'doubts' that he could afford to give free rein to his ruthless, sceptical intelligence on all matters that seemed to be of comparatively superficial importance—religious, political or scientific. As he expressed himself in speech and writing with clarity, candour, and a natural tendency to epigram that he had consciously to curb, he often gave an impression of flippancy and cynicism that made him many enemies.

More important, his faith gave him an unusual freedom from conventional doubts and fears. Once when he was Foreign Secretary at a moment of acute international crisis, he expressed his relief at the departure of some guests, who had kindly condoled with him on the burden of his responsibility. For he said he did not know what to say to them, as he really did not know what they meant. When his family protested, 'he proceeded to explain further', as Lady Gwendolen Cecil relates in her biography of her father (vol. 1, p. 119). 'He was about to start upon a walk and was standing at the moment at the open door, looking out upon the threatening clouds of an autumn afternoon. "I don't understand," he repeated, "what people mean when they talk of the burden of responsibility. I should understand if they spoke of the burden of decision—I feel it now, trying to make up my mind whether or no to take a greatcoat with me. I feel it in exactly the same way, but no more, when I am writing a despatch upon which peace or war may depend. Its degree depends upon the materials for decision that are available and not in the least upon the magnitude of the results which may follow." Then, after a moment's pause and in a lower tone, he added, "With the results I have nothing to do."'

It comes as no surprise that he was sceptical of all 'Plans', alliances, leagues and grandiose schemes of improvement; both in home and foreign affairs he preferred to deal with events as they came, on the strength of the evidence available and to the best of his ability.

His self-reliance and independence in the conduct of foreign policy were very marked. They revealed themselves immediately on his appointment as Foreign Secretary in 1878, when he sat up till three in the morning composing the note to the Powers (The Salisbury Circular) that they at once recognised as a sign that a new, strong hand was on the reins. It was typical of his method of working. He never went to the Foreign Office before lunch. He worked at home, in London or at Hatfield, in his study behind double doors so constructed that from within he could not hear a knock on the outer door. All he had to do was lock the outer door and he could work undisturbed until he was finished. He respected and trusted his subordinates in all matters within their competence. He went to great lengths to explain his policy to his ambassadors, but he expected clear, accurate information from them, not advice. *He* was responsible for policy, and *he* formulated it.

Could this aloofness, this detachment, this solitary method of working be partly responsible for a later impression of isolation in Britain's position? If so, it was reinforced by the international ?(CR.mEA) situation in Salisbury's time. Between the Franco-Prussian War of 1870 and the First World War there was no major European war and consequently no peace conference. Apart from the Berlin Africa Conference (1884) to settle the problems of the Congo, the only major conference was the Congress of Berlin (1878), at which Salisbury made his bow as Foreign Secretary. From then until his final resignation in 1900 there was no other such international meeting. Negotiations were conducted in writing.

The international situation may perhaps have favoured an impression of relative detachment from the affairs of Europe; the fundamentals of British foreign policy remained unchanged. In an article in *The Listener* of 20 May 1948 Sir Charles Webster enumerated them thus: Britain's insular position; Britain's naval power; a determination that Europe should not be dominated by any one Power; industry and trade as the bases of Britain's power, from which grew the Empire; an interest in preserving world peace; an interest in the spread of independent nations with democratic institutions.

In this period Britain's insular position remained unchanged. The position of the navy did not. From the replacement of wooden ships by ironclads in the sixties there was continuous technical change initiated by improvements in guns. This was much to Britain's disadvantage. Wooden ships took a long time to build and, once built, lasted for sixty years. Given her fleet in being, Britain could hardly be overtaken by any Power wishing to rival it. But with the invention of new and more powerful guns, and the development of stronger armour to resist them, ships became obsolete within a generation. H.M.S. *Rodney* of the Admiral class, launched in 1884, could, if properly handled, have sent the entire fleet of ironclads to the bottom; and a fleet of the Magnificent class, laid down in 1895, could comfortably have put paid to a fleet of 'Admirals'. This situation meant that any Power could compete with Britain if it had the resources and the will. In 1888 there was a scare that France and Russia would combine their fleets in the Mediterranean and make the position of the British Mediterranean fleet impossible. As a result the Naval Intelligence Division of the Admiralty and an independent report by three admirals pointed out that, in the event of war, the British fleet would be in a position of inferiority to the combined French and Russian fleets. At the same time Bismarck for his own reasons urged that Britain should strengthen her fleet. This combined pressure converted Salisbury and the Cabinet to the view that Britain should adopt the two-Power standard, i.e. her fleet should outnumber those of any two Powers combined. This policy was embodied in the Naval Defence Act (1889), which fixed the ratios at 6 to 5 for first-class ships and 4½ to 2 for second-class ships. As C. J. Lowe points out in his *Salisbury and the Mediterranean* (p. 44), this was the foundation of British naval policy till 1921.

Between 1871 and 1890 there was no great danger of any one Power dominating Europe. Germany was the strongest Power, but as long as Bismarck was Chancellor there was no risk of an aggressive foreign policy designed to impose German wishes on Europe by force. Bismarck's policy was pacific and conservative.

He had brought the German Empire into being by diplomacy and war; he wanted to maintain its position and his own. In his own words, 'Try to be *à trois* in a world governed by five Powers': Germany, Austria-Hungary, Russia, France, Britain. He made sure of this in a series of agreements: the Dual Alliance with Austria-Hungary (1879), the League of the Three Emperors (the *Dreikaiserbund*) (1881), the Reinsurance Treaty with Russia (1887) and the association of Italy with Germany and Austria-Hungary in the Triple Alliance (1882), for what it was worth. After Bismarck's fall Kaiser William II introduced a marked element of impulsiveness and instability into foreign affairs, but Germany constituted no great threat to the balance of power or to vital British interests until the expansion of the German navy from 1898 onwards.

The maintenance of British industry and trade was closely linked with the preservation of world peace. A short, local war might bring economic gain, as did, for example, the China wars of the forties and fifties or the Spanish-American War of 1898; but a world war, especially a prolonged one, would dislocate the international commercial and monetary mechanism and thereby cause untold damage to the British economy and perhaps even undermine the position of London as the world's monetary centre. Seen the other way round, through the eyes of Cobdenite orthodoxy, international trade prevented the outbreak of war and furthered international peace. There was sound historical foundation for this view, in that the international economic order had provided the nations of Europe with untold opportunities for economic expansion throughout the world and had contained their national aspirations within its framework. Salisbury was willing to impose a limit to the advance of foreign Powers in Asia and Africa, if necessary by force, but it was his constant endeavour to adjust matters so as to prevent these clashes from adversely affecting British interests in Europe or leading to a world war. His diplomacy was continuously at work in the Near East and Africa.

2 The Near East question A crucial area for trade and for imperial power was India and China, for trade with these two

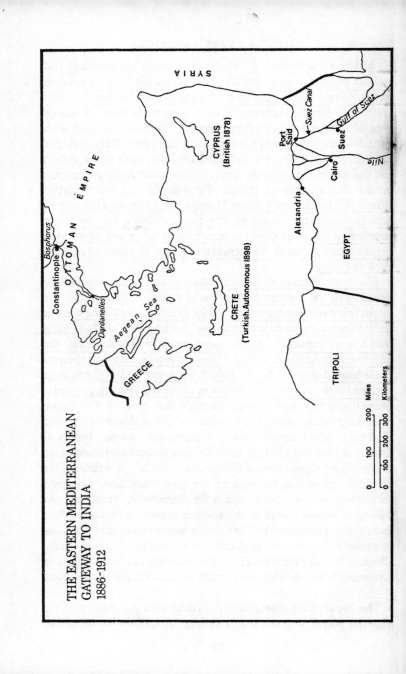

THE EASTERN MEDITERRANEAN
GATEWAY TO INDIA
1886-1912

countries represented almost a quarter of Britain's entire exports, while China and Japan imported more from Britain than from the whole of the rest of the world. India was the focus of British power in the east, with supporting points at Hong Kong and Singapore. Between Waterloo and the Franco-Prussian War there was no serious external threat to India. The French had been conquered and the Russian advance into central Asia and Siberia had hardly begun. It was only in the last quarter of the century that danger arose again with French activity in Indo-China and Russian eastward expansion. But France was much more menacing in Africa, and Salisbury was not disposed to take the Russian threat to India too seriously, though he was ready to stop the Russians occupying Herat in Afghanistan even at the risk of war.

Very different were the routes to the east via the Cape and the Mediterranean. These were vital. Britain had bought the Cape from Holland in 1815 as the indispensable port of call on the ocean route to India. Ever since, the need to control Cape Colony had governed British relations with the Boers who were already settled there.

Even more important after the opening of the Suez Canal in 1869 was the Mediterranean route. Before then the route that ran across Syria and down the Euphrates to the Persian Gulf was an important complement to the ocean route round the Cape. British politicians and officials shared Napoleon's view that Constantinople was 'the Key to India', and it was British policy to keep Turkey in being and to ensure that she retained possession of Constantinople and the Straits (the Bosphorus and the Dardanelles). This involved constant alertness to any threat from Russia. Historians have generally supported this view and regarded it as axiomatic that it was in Britain's interests to back Turkey and contain Russia's land and sea forces. There was force in this view before 1869, but it was much weakened by the cutting of the Suez Canal. As Robert Blake points out in his life of Disraeli it is almost a thousand miles by sea from Constantinople to Port Said and a good deal more by land.

Salisbury himself was sceptical of the dogma that Constantinople was 'the Key to India' and of the Russian threat to India from central Asia, and remarked that much of the trouble came from British politicians using maps on too small a scale. Nevertheless, when he succeeded Derby as Foreign Secretary in the middle of the Near East crisis of 1878, he carried out the policy of Disraeli and the Foreign Office to the best of his ability; and as late as 1886 he wrote in a memorandum to the Austrian foreign minister: 'For a clearly defined object such as the defence of Constantinople, England no doubt would fight.' But by then events had a good deal altered Salisbury's angle of vision.

In the first place it was an assumption of British policy that the Sultan relied as much on British support as Britain relied on Turkish independence. Turkey controlled the Straits in peace and war, and in any crisis the Sultan's first thought was to call on the British fleet to protect his capital and his person. By 1885 this was no longer true; there was now much less disposition to rely exclusively on Britain. This put the use of the British fleet in quite a new light. Instead of being called up to Constantinople it might have to force a passage through the Dardanelles. Admiralty opinion was doubtful if this could be done without disproportionate losses. Furthermore there seemed to have been a shift of Russian interest away from the Balkans towards central Asia. If this was indeed so, it would take the pressure off Turkey and make a Russian attempt to occupy Constantinople less likely.

All this affected Salisbury's policy in the Bulgarian crisis that broke out in 1885. The Bulgarians of Eastern Rumelia joined themselves to the new Bulgarian state with the enthusiastic support of Prince Alexander of Bulgaria and in clear breach of the *Treaty of Berlin* (1878). Salisbury thought it important for the Concert of Europe to act on a breach of a major European treaty and especially on one of so recent a date. He also feared independent action by the Tsar in Bulgaria and at Constantinople. Accordingly from the first he promoted vigorous diplomatic action through the ambassadors at Constantinople. Thanks to the military successes of the Bulgarian army and their effect in swinging Bismarck round to support of Salisbury's policy, an agreement recognising the union of the two provinces was reached in January 1886.

Tsar Alexander III approved the agreement, but the danger of Russian intervention was not over. The Russians forced the abdication of Prince Alexander and then sent a Russian general to take control. The Bulgars would not submit to this, and they were backed up in varying degrees by Austria-Hungary, Britain and France. There was for many months a real risk of war. But in the end the Tsar accepted the prince whom the Bulgars had chosen as their ruler, Ferdinand of Coburg, and he remained on the throne till 1918. The Russian army did not invade. Why not? It is not certain. The Bulgarian army had shown impressive discipline and ability in war. The war party in Austria had made a good deal of noise. Bismarck, Salisbury and the French from different angles had worked for peace. But perhaps A. J. P. Taylor has come nearest the truth when he writes (p. 323): 'There was a deeper cause still. The Russians regarded the Balkans with indifference or even dislike; their ambition turned towards central Asia and the Far East. They wanted security at the Straits; and they resented the offence to their prestige in Bulgaria. But they would make no serious move, unless assured of German neutrality.'

At the time the Russian attitude was less clear. Salisbury summed up his policy as based on the threat of Russian physical and moral advance in the Balkans, because this 'threatens our communications with our Eastern possessions, and may directly and indirectly shake our power over our Mahometan subjects'. The goal of British policy remained the same: the safety of the Mediterranean route to the east. But circumstances were changing, and Salisbury was adjusting the details of his policy to meet them. Events in Bulgaria had already convinced him that Disraeli and he had been wrong in 1878 to fear that a big Bulgaria would be a Russian satellite, which would grant the Russians a naval base on the Aegean. 'Evidence had accumulated [during 1886]', writes Lady Gwendolen Cecil (vol. III, p. 246), 'both as to the wishes of the population and the reality of the authority which their chosen ruler exercised over them—even to the point of securing unbroken peace in the frontier villages. For a Balkan population to accept restraint from raiding indicated a very absolute submission.' Salisbury respected this evidence and worked to secure the approval of the Powers for a united Bulgaria, with Eastern Rumelia joined to the original principality of Bulgaria. Salisbury had not, like Palmerston or Gladstone, a sympathy for constitutional states, based on temperament and political philosophy alike, but he had been revolted in 1876-7 by Turkish cruelty and misgovernment, and he was now. So were his fellow-countrymen. 'Patriotic suspicion of Russia', to quote Lady Gwendolen again, 'and sympathy with the subject races of Turkey were alike gratified by his championship of Prince Alexander and the Bulgarians.' Self-interest and sympathy marched hand in hand. For it seemed that a series of autonomous Balkan states might constitute the best barrier to Russian advance and perhaps even the best buttress of a crumbling Turkey. 'Sir William White's idea of "the Balkans for the Balkan peoples" was substantially that of Salisbury,' write Harold Temperley and Lillian Penson in *Foundations of British Foreign Policy* (C.U.P. 1938, p. 431, n.), 'and he [Salisbury] applied it to Bulgaria at this time.'

But Salisbury was more sceptical than before of the Sultan's will and power to resist Russian domination. To reinforce these and to ensure the Mediterranean as far as possible against the consequences of any further weakening of the Sultan's power was the object of the two Mediterranean Agreements that Salisbury concluded with Italy and Austria in 1887. The first Mediterranean Agreement was based on Italy's determination not to have Britain as an enemy on any account, and on her desire for British support against France, with whom relations were very bad after the French occupation of Tunis in 1881. British relations with France were also bad on account of Egypt (see p. 22), and there was some nervousness at the Admiralty over the possible junction of the French and Russian fleets in the Mediterranean in the event of war. Salisbury decided to turn these feelings to account and to bring about a general security agreement for the Mediterranean. In the secret convention signed by Italy and Britain on 12 February, to which Austria-Hungary adhered in an exchange of notes on 24 March, the Powers undertook to uphold the *status quo* in the Mediterranean, the Adriatic, the Aegean and the Black Sea. Italy accepted the British position in Egypt. Britain agreed to support Italy in the event of 'encroachments' in N. Africa by another Power (which could only be France). They would make a common front if Turkey, and specially Constantinople, were threatened; and probably if Austria-Hungary alone were attacked by Russia. In no circumstances would Britain take part in an offensive war against France. By the Second Mediterranean Agreement of 12 December 1887, set out like the first in a secret interchange of notes, the three Powers, Austria-Hungary, Britain and Italy, agreed to maintain peace, the *status quo* in the East and the Balkans, and 'Turkish independence and integrity'. But their lack of confidence in the Sultan is revealed in the last two clauses. Clause 8 provides that in the event of Turkish complicity in any illegal enterprise affecting Bulgaria or the Straits the Powers will provisionally occupy such points of territory as may be necessary 'to secure the objects determined by previous Treaties'. The last clause lays down that none of the Powers shall reveal the existence or the contents of the agreement to Turkey or to any other Power without the previous agreement of all three Powers.

In the event the Powers were not called upon to act on the terms of the agreement. By the next Turkish crisis in 1895 the situation in Turkey and in Europe had changed again. In Turkey itself the Sultan had once more shown the character of his rule. Alarmed by signs of increased national feeling among the Armenian citizens of his empire he had instigated the massacre first of Armenian peasants in the east and then of Armenians in Constantinople and in several towns in Asia Minor. In Europe the new German emperor, Kaiser William II, had dismissed Bismarck in 1890 and decided in the same year not to renew the Reinsurance Treaty with Russia. This led to a new fluidity in European relations and eventually to the Franco-Russian understanding of 1891, the military convention of 1892 and finally the alliance of 1894.

These events altered the whole aspect of the Mediterranean, Turkey and the Straits. In the first place, by the time of his return to office in 1895, Salisbury's doubts about the Sultan's ability to govern had deepened into a conviction that Turkey was near dissolution. This conviction, proved wrong by the events of 1897 and later admitted to be wrong by Salisbury himself, nevertheless played an important part in determining his policy in the years 1895–7. Secondly British opinion, though not as outraged by the Armenian massacres as it had been by the Bulgarian atrocities twenty years before, was outspokenly hostile to the Sultan, nor was there any jingoist swing back in his favour as there had been in 1878. Thirdly the Sultan himself had reversed his traditional policy of reliance on Britain: what had been feared by the Powers in the Second Mediterranean Agreement had come to pass. The outward and visible sign of this was to be seen in the Straits—the fortification of the Dardanelles and the neglect of the fortifications of the Bosphorus.

At the same time the Franco-Russian alliance had reinforced the Admiralty's fears of joint action by the French and Russian fleets in the Mediterranean. It was confirmed in its opinion that it would be impossible to force the Dardanelles without unacceptable losses and further reported that it would be necessary to 'neutralise' the French Toulon fleet before attempting the operation. Salisbury, as always sceptical of expert opinion, did not share the Admiralty view, but the Cabinet did and was unwilling to risk going it alone. In the circumstances there was nothing that Salisbury could do but try for a concerted European policy. But whereas in 1885 the key to success was Bismarck's support, in 1895 it was the Tsar's.

The acute phase of the crisis opened with the massacre of the Armenians in Constantinople in broad daylight on 26 and 27 August 1896. A Russian threat of bombardment forced the Sultan to order the massacres to stop. But the danger of further outrages and further independent Russian action remained. Tsar Nicholas II was paying a private visit to his wife's grandmother, Queen Victoria, at Balmoral in September. Salisbury took the opportunity to have two long conversations with him in private. In these he suggested concerted action by the Powers to force the Sultan to reform, backed by an ultimatum that they would force him to abdicate if he did not carry out what the Powers put forward. He went on with boldness and some indiscretion to explain that Britain's interest in the Straits was now only secondary, for their control was no longer vital for the defence of the route to India, but that Britain must stand by her ally Austria-Hungary who was still vitally concerned: Austria would of course demand security in the event of a Russian control of the Straits, but might it not be possible for the two governments to work out some scheme satisfactory to them both? The Tsar was taken aback and said it was best to preserve the *status quo*. In fact the Russian and Austrian governments had already secretly agreed to preserve the *status quo* for the time being or, in the contemporary phrase, 'to put the Balkan question on ice'. The reason for this was the Russian expansion into Siberia and consequently sharpened interest in the Far East. But as so often there was a conflict between the Tsar's advisers, and as usual Nicholas II could not make up his mind. In the end the Far Easterners won and the Tsar sent instructions to his ambassador in Constantinople to preserve the sultanate and to work with the other ambassadors to devise a means of enforcing effective reform on the Sultan. In February they reached agreement to set up and support a supreme council of state to supervise the Turkish administration. But in the event it never came into being. In April the Greeks invaded Turkey. To everyone's astonishment they were soundly beaten and by the end of the month routed. The Powers intervened to save them from their folly: they prevented the Turks taking advantage of their victory to regain land inhabited by Christians, and declared Crete autonomous under Prince George of Greece. The Turks had nevertheless shown that the sultanate was not on the verge of dissolution, but was still capable of giving a good account of itself. The reforms and the supreme council were relegated to limbo.

In the course of the crisis British policy had made a decisive shift: Salisbury had written off Constantinople. When the Austrian foreign minister Goluchowski tried to link the renewal of the Mediterranean Agreements with a British pledge to defend Constantinople, Salisbury refused to give it. Thereupon Austria-Hungary refused to renew the agreements, and they lapsed in 1897. From then on it ceased to be British policy to defend Constantinople and the Straits at all costs. They were no longer vital to the defence of the route to India. This could be defended equally well from Egypt.

3 The Nile and tropical Africa ~~The defence~~ of the route to India had originally drawn Britain into Egypt. In 1876 the bankruptcy of the Khedive of Egypt had lured the French government into action to protect the shareholders of the Suez Canal Company and the bondholders of Egypt's £90 million debt. Britain dared not let France act alone. As Salisbury put it, 'You may renounce—or monopolise—or share. Renouncing would have been to place the French across our road to India. Monopolising would have been very near the risk of war. So we resolved to share.' So Anglo-French financial control was established. Then the nationalist revolt in 1881 and the French withdrawal in 1882 left Britain in unwilling, and supposedly temporary, occupation.

Occupation was a perpetual embarrassment. France remained in a state of self-pitying resentment, sore at having withdrawn and jealous of the British still being there. With France in this state of mind, cordial relations were impossible. This friction and the existence from 1885 of the international *Caisse de la Dette Publique* into which the Egyptian revenue was paid gave Germany a handle that Bismarck used against Britain with unscrupulous skill to extract concessions in the colonial field and to remind British governments of their dependence on German goodwill. On the other hand withdrawal was difficult. The country's upper class, the pashas, were foreigners in Egypt; they were as unpopular as they were incompetent. The defeat of the nationalist revolt had broken the power and authority of the native Egyptian soldiers who might have provided an alternative ruling class. There remained the peasants. Withdrawal it seemed would lead either to anarchy or to occupation by another Power, probably France; neither could be contemplated.

A possible way out of this impasse suggested itself: to persuade the Sultan, the legal suzerain of Egypt, to exercise his authority in practice. In 1885 Salisbury sent Sir Henry Drummond Wolff as a special envoy to Constantinople to work for the evacuation of Egypt in agreement with the Sultan 'with certain privileges reserved for England'. On this occasion he was unsuccessful. But Wolff went again to Constantinople in 1887 and negotiated a convention that was signed on 22 May. It provided for the withdrawal of British troops within three years, but also for the postponement of withdrawal if necessary, and for their return 'if order and security in the interior were disturbed'.

Unfortunately this convention was signed while the jingoist movement in France led by General Boulanger was at its height, and it was impossible for any French politician to defy public opinion and accept it. The French government combined with the Tsar to force the Sultan to revoke it. Bismarck indicated his support for Britain. British troops stayed in Egypt. Salisbury concluded that he must continue his policy of cautious alignment with Germany and her allies in the Triple Alliance. The French soon regretted their action, but by then it was too late to reverse their policy. However much they might hanker after Britain as an ally, they were stuck with the Tsar. 'The failure of the Drummond Wolff convention', writes A. J. P. Taylor, 'was the decisive factor in sending the French along the road to alliance with Russia.' It was also the decisive factor in making the British occupation of Egypt not merely temporary, but semi-permanent.

On behalf of the British and Egyptian governments Evelyn Baring, later Lord Cromer, took a firm grip on the administration with the double object of making the Khedive solvent, thereby securing the rights of the holders of Egyptian government bonds, and of making Egypt a safe base for the route to India. By 1890 he had achieved his first aim: there was a surplus of £E 591,000, and from then on the surplus increased annually. The security problem remained.

In the 1880s and 1890s the danger to Egypt from the north was adequately contained: by the Mediterranean Agreements, by the British fleet, based from 1889 onwards on the two-Power standard, and by the continued existence of Turkey, which, as we have seen, belied Salisbury's pessimism by her conduct in 1897. The more threatening danger came from the south, from the upper Nile. 'The Nile is the life of Egypt', wrote Riaz Pasha to Cromer; 'the Nile means the Soudan.' All was well so long as the upper Nile was in the hands of untutored natives; danger would threaten if it fell into the hands of a Power equipped with the resources of modern technology. 'The savages of the Soudan',

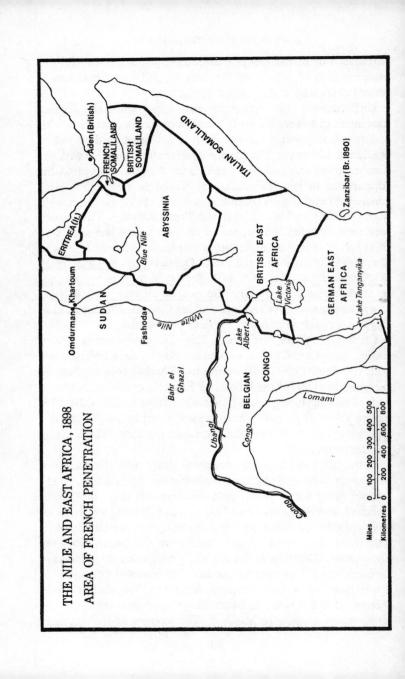

THE NILE AND EAST AFRICA, 1898
AREA OF FRENCH PENETRATION

Aden (British)
FRENCH SOMALILAND
BRITISH SOMALILAND
ITALIAN SOMALILAND
ERITREA (It.)
Zanzibar (Br. 1890)
Omdurman Khartoum
SUDAN
Blue Nile
ABYSSINIA
BRITISH EAST AFRICA
Fashoda
White Nile
Lake Victoria
GERMAN EAST AFRICA
Lake Tanganyika
Bahr el Ghazal
Lake Albert
CONGO
BELGIAN CONGO
Lomami
Ubangi
Congo
Congo

Miles 0 100 200 300 400 500
Kilometres 0 200 400 600 800

wrote Lord Milner in *England in Egypt*, 1892, pp. 197–8, 'may never themselves possess sufficient engineering skill to play tricks with the Nile, but ... it is an uncomfortable thought that the regular supply of water by the great river, which is to Egypt not a question of convenience and prosperity, but actually of life, must always be exposed to some risk, as long as the upper reaches of that river are not under Egyptian control. Who can say what might happen, if some day a civilised Power, or a Power commanding civilised skill, were to undertake great engineering works on the Upper Nile, and to divert for the artificial irrigation of that region the water which is essential for the artificial irrigation of Egypt?'

There were two main branches of the upper Nile, the Blue Nile and the White Nile, rising respectively in the highlands of Abyssinia and in Lake Victoria. The ruler of Abyssinia, Menelek, was powerful and intelligent. Adventurers and promoters of all kinds were active at his capital and the French were assiduous in courting his favour. Salisbury sent an envoy in 1896 to try and keep Menelek neutral in relation to Anglo-French rivalry, but he found the French had been beforehand and secured a treaty establishing Abyssinian rights to territory on the right bank of the Nile south of Khartoum and French rights to the territory facing it on the left bank. The Italians too were interested in expanding towards the upper Nile from the Red Sea, and Salisbury encouraged them to penetrate far enough inland to create a buffer between Abyssinia and the Sudan.

Lake Victoria lay in the hinterland of the territory of the Sultan of Zanzibar. In the early 1880s there had been much British and German rivalry on the coast and in penetrating inland. Bismarck had eventually taken up the German cause and forced the Sultan of Zanzibar and the Gladstone government in 1885 to concede rights to Germany over a large area westward of Zanzibar (roughly the mainland territory of the present state of Tanzania). But the boundaries of British and German East Africa as far inland as Lake Victoria were still unmapped. Salisbury was determined to secure the still undefined area round Lake Victoria and so prevent Germany or any other Power placing itself on the source of the

White Nile. He was making cautious progress towards an agreement with Bismarck when the latter was suddenly dismissed by Kaiser William II. Salisbury immediately took advantage of the new Chancellor's wish for a successful stroke in the field of foreign affairs and pressed forward the negotiations. They reached a rapid conclusion in the Anglo-German Convention (1890). By this Germany recognised as British the area round Lake Victoria (more or less the modern Uganda and Kenya), and the island of Zanzibar. In return Britain conceded Germany access to the Zambesi from German S.W. Africa by a narrow strip of land (the Caprivi Strip or Tail); and ceded the island of Heligoland, some thirty miles off the North Sea coast of Germany. The convention was unpopular in both countries; each thought it had been done down by the other. It is clear that Britain gained in Africa. But there has been a good deal of controversy over the value of Heligoland. It is true that Germany fortified it and that in the Second World War it was a strong submarine and anti-aircraft base. But is it credible that Britain could have held it in a war with Germany under twentieth-century conditions?

The Anglo-German Convention was supplemented by agreements with Portugal and France. There had been friction with Portugal for some time, for she was vaguely interested in linking up her colony in west Africa (Angola) with that in east Africa (Mozambique), though her claims to inland territory were in Salisbury's word 'archaeological'—another case of maps on too small a scale? Patience and firmness won the day. Agreement was reached in 1890 and embodied in a convention in 1891. Portugal recognised the British position in Mashonaland and Nyasaland, while Britain recognised a Portuguese sphere of influence inland from Mozambique much wider than before.

France had claims in east and west Africa which she pressed with some vigour after the signature of the Anglo-German Convention. She was in a strong position to do this, as she had been a signatory of the original treaty with the Sultan of Zanzibar governing the mainland territory west of Zanzibar. Salisbury regarded the claims as exorbitant and fought a lengthy battle to reduce them. Eventually in the Anglo-French Convention (1890)

26

Britain recognised the French possession of Madagascar and France recognised the British possession of Zanzibar and Nigeria.

Rosebery completed Salisbury's work. Archibald Philip Primrose, 5th Earl of Rosebery (1847–1929), Whig aristocrat, millionaire, wit, connoisseur of 18th century literature, keen shot and racegoer, who won the Derby twice, was an imperialist who followed Salisbury's policy. As Queen Victoria's nominee as Foreign Secretary in Gladstone's government of 1892 and as the indispensable guarantor of the unity of the Liberal Party, severely strained by Gladstone's Home Rule policy, Rosebery was able to *IMPORTANT* get his way with his reluctant colleagues. He forced them to annex Uganda, which formally became a protectorate of the crown by the British Uganda Protectorate Treaty (1894). He further signed an agreement with King Leopold of the Belgians, the Anglo-Congolese Treaty (1894), designed to seal off the upper Nile from French expansion from west Africa. But this was a dead letter, for French and German hostility forced Leopold to abandon the treaty. The Sudan remained open to penetration from the west. But the British government, in the person of Sir Edward Grey, Parliamentary Under-Secretary for Foreign Affairs, gave a public warning to France, in a speech in the House of Commons, that it regarded the upper Nile as an Anglo-Egyptian sphere and would look on a French expedition to it as 'an unfriendly act' (the so-called Grey Declaration).

Since 1883 the Sudan, conquered earlier in the century for Egypt by Mehemet Ali, had been in the hands of the Dervishes, led first by the Mahdi and then by his son the Khalifa. This suited Britain, as it meant that there was no serious threat to the life of Egypt while Cromer was consolidating his administration. But it was not a situation likely to last indefinitely. Salisbury intended to reconquer the Sudan for Egypt when opportunity offered. Meanwhile he had given himself as much freedom of action as possible by the series of agreements with France, Germany and Portugal described above.

His hand was forced by the unexpected collapse of the Italians in east Africa, their army being routed by the Abyssinians at the battle of Adowa on 1 March 1896. Italy no longer covered the south-eastern flank of the Sudan, and the way was open to an Abyssinian advance towards the Nile at Khartoum. Later in the same year the French government despatched Colonel Marchand to west Africa to undertake an expedition up the Congo and Ubangi rivers towards the White Nile. He was to march through the Bahr-el-Ghazal, making treaties with native chiefs as he went, to stake out French claims to the territory west of the White Nile and finally to plant the French flag on the banks of the river itself. Salisbury at first tried to forestall Marchand by organising an expedition from Uganda, but this was frustrated by the mutiny of the Sudanese garrison in Uganda and by a rebellion there. There was nothing for it but to order the re-conquest of the Sudan from Egypt. Against the wishes of Cromer Salisbury did this in March 1896. The original intention was to advance only as far as Dongola and see how things went. But Kitchener's rout of the Dervishes at Atbara on 8 April 1898 and the strong rumours of Marchand's approach from the west determined the despatch of British troops to ensure complete victory and the occupation of the whole of the Sudan. On 2 September Kitchener again defeated the Dervishes and immediately occupied Omdurman and Khartoum. Three days later came the news that half-a-dozen white men and a detachment of black troops had run up their flag at Fashoda 500 miles up the river. These were Marchand, his officers and some hundred Senegalese soldiers. Kitchener met them at Fashoda on 19 September. He was courteous but firm. He hoisted the Egyptian flag and when he departed left a garrison behind. Tension was high between France and Britain for months. But it did not lead to war. Salisbury was as courteous as Kitchener but as firm. He held all the cards. Neither Germany nor Russia would move a soldier or a ship to help France. The British fleet was superior to the French in numbers and in readiness. The French foreign minister Delcassé was a realist and gave Marchand instructions to withdraw on 4 November. In due course the Anglo-French Convention (1899) fixed the boundary of the French and British spheres to coincide more or less with the watershed of the Congo and the Nile. Britain had beaten off all comers, taken control of the upper Nile on behalf of Egypt and ensured its life and safety.

4 Salisbury and splendid isolation In a speech at Lewes on 26 February 1896 in defence of the government's foreign policy Goschen, the First Lord of the Admiralty, after noting the need for negotiation and for vigilant defence, went on to refer to Britain's isolation. 'Our isolation', he said, 'if isolation it be, was self-imposed. It arose out of our unwillingness to take part in Bismarck's "log-rolling" system. We are not good at the game. We have been asked to play it, but we do not like the game, and so, while they are all bartering favour for favour, promise for promise, we have stood alone in that which is called isolation— our splendid isolation, as one of our Colonial friends was good enough to call it. Let us look the matter in the face. We cannot make alliances unless we are prepared to give as well as to receive. . . . Why are we isolated? We are isolated because we will not promise things which possibly we might be unwilling to perform. We are isolated possibly because we do not wish to take part in certain proceedings. But if it comes to some of these great questions that might strike at our great power, our life, our influence, I do not believe we should find ourselves without allies.' From this it is clear that Goschen thought Britain's isolation far from complete.

In March 1898 Joseph Chamberlain remarked that 'isolation, or at least non-entanglement in alliances' had been British policy for years. If isolation is taken to be 'non-entanglement in alliances' this is not only true but a truism. From the Congress of Vienna onwards Britain had followed a policy of detachment from the Continent, and with very few exceptions made alliances only in wartime. But in fact in 1898 Britain was in a state of isolation that went far beyond non-entanglement. This had first been revealed by President Cleveland of the United States. On 17 December 1895 he had sent a message to Congress about the long-standing boundary dispute between Venezuela and British Guiana. In this he invoked the Monroe Doctrine as a ground for his decision to appoint an American commission to define the boundary and to impose its award on Britain, by war if necessary. American opinion exploded with delight and the Powers looked on with malicious glee. By contrast British opinion was calm and even indifferent. Salisbury was able to co-operate with the commission in its investigations during 1896, and by the Treaty of Washington (1897) the matter was referred to arbitration. The arbitrators' award in 1899 confirmed all the main British claims. This was satisfactory. Much more satisfactory was the development of a good understanding between Britain and the U.S.A. and the improvement of their relations at a time when the U.S.A. was emerging as a major Power. Salisbury was careful to foster this atmosphere by indicating his support for the U.S.A. in the Spanish-American War of 1898.

Meantime another episode had revealed British isolation in a more lurid light. On 29 December 1895 Jameson launched his 'Raid' on the Transvaal. By 2 January 1896 the raiders were trapped and had to lay down their arms. Next day the Kaiser cabled his congratulations to President Kruger on having dealt with 'the armed hordes which as disturbers of the peace broke into your country' and on having preserved the independence of the Transvaal. The Kruger Telegram touched the British on the raw; it was indeed a bitter symbol of the attitude of the Powers. Events in the Far East in 1897 (see p. 44) and in the Sudan in 1898 (see p. 28) confirmed Britain's isolation.

Despite this the phrase 'splendid isolation' did not at once gain currency, least of all as a shorthand description of Salisbury's foreign policy between 1886 and the outbreak of the South African War in 1899. It does not appear in Justin McCarthy's *History of Our Own Times* (1897) nor in Herbert Paul's *History of Modern England* (1906). The obituary of Salisbury in *The Times* of Monday, 24 August 1903 makes no mention of it, and summarises his foreign policy in these words: 'Abroad, to maintain the rights of England firmly and discreetly, while strictly respecting the rights of other nations; never to forget the appalling cost and the dread uncertainty of modern wars, and to make every effort for the preservation of peace, whether by mutual concessions or by maintaining in times of crisis the co-operation of the Powers, the "inchoate federation of Europe"—such were the elements of Lord Salisbury's policy.' The article on Salisbury in the *Dictionary of National Biography* (published 1912) takes much the same line, but referring to the Armenian Question notes that Salisbury would not act without the approval of the Powers—'of the "Concert of Europe", an expression which in his time became very familiar.'

It does not seem to be until after the First World War that the phrase appears in print as a description of Salisbury's foreign policy. W. H. Dawson, writing on the second and third Salisbury administrations in the *Cambridge History of Foreign Policy*, Vol. III (1923), pp. 260–1, says: 'His caution was strikingly shown in his attitude to coalitions and alliances. Tempted more than once, by a statesman whose confidence was supposed to be the highest form of flattery, to consider offers of the kind, he listened politely and as politely declined, yet weakening no friendship because of his preference for the old national attitude of "splendid isolation".' Evidence of a similar view is the title given to Volume I of *British Documents on the Origins of the War, 1898–1914: The end of British isolation*, published in 1926.

Salisbury was certainly not an isolationist 'in the sense of avoiding every form of contact with foreign nations'. Nor did he conceive himself to be carrying out a policy of isolation. The *Annual Register* for 1878 quotes him as saying, 'For a short time there have been men, eminent in public affairs, who have tried to persuade you that all the past history of England was a mistake— that the duty of England, the interests of England, was to confine herself solely to her own insular forces, to cultivate commerce, to accumulate riches, and not, it was said, to entangle herself in foreign policies. They were men who disdained empire, who objected to colonies, and who grumbled even at the possession of India. . . . The commerce of a great commercial country like this will only flourish—history attests it again and again—under the shadow of empire, and those who give up empire in order to make commerce prosper will end by losing both.' This passage, in its sentiments if not in its wording, might have been uttered by Palmerston. It may fairly stand as an expression of Salisbury's point of view throughout his long career, and it gives substance to the judgement of Ronald Robinson and John Gallagher, that 'under Salisbury's direction British policy . . . acquired . . . a certain brilliance of formulation; but its concepts remained essentially the same as of old'.

How then did it come about that the label 'splendid isolation' was pinned on it? W. H. Dawson himself suggests one possible reason. He writes that under Salisbury the country was no longer agitated by 'spirited foreign policy', for Salisbury's policy was one of 'intelligent inaction', or in his own words, 'maintaining things as they are'. The contrast he intends is no doubt immediately with the *forward* policy of Disraeli, but it could be extended to the policy of Palmerston, which was nothing if not spirited; and it is possible that some twentieth century historians have unconsciously made this extension and, in so doing, come to think of Salisbury's policy as isolationist in a way that Palmerston's was not.

Another possible explanation may lie in the areas with which policy had to concern itself. For Palmerston these were largely in Europe; and he made his greatest contributions to foreign policy in Belgium and the Near East. Already in Disraeli's time policy was much concerned with areas outside Europe, and it is incontestable that Salisbury was as much concerned with Africa as Europe, and he was also involved with America and the Far East. Foreign policy remains foreign policy, whether it is dealing with Africa, America, Asia or Europe. Because India was the concern of the India Office in the first place, and the Cape and the Niger of the Colonial Office, events in the colonies, and so by extension all over Africa, may be thought of as belonging to the sphere of colonial rather than of foreign policy. Looked at from this point of view there may appear to be much less *foreign* policy in the last quarter of the century than there had been in any other. This is an illusion. The Transvaal concerned the Foreign Office as much as the Colonial Office; the Nile was as important in Salisbury's foreign policy as the Rhine. But it is an illusion that may have distorted historians' vision.

An even more likely distortion was produced by the First World War and the search for its causes. Historians looked at the events before the war as events leading up to it. They could not help seeing that in the first decade of the twentieth century Europe divided into two camps. Britain was associated with one of the camps by the ententes with France and Russia. In retrospect entente seemed inevitably to have led to alliance; in retrospect the period immediately before the entente seemed, by contrast, more fluid and open, and British policy seemed detached to the point of isolation.

Chapter II

The changing situation

1 New forces All points in time may be, as Ranke remarked, equidistant from eternity, but they are not equidistant from one another; and the view of a point or a tract of time may vary a good deal with the viewpoint. So a particular period of history may appear static and tranquil to the historian of some of its aspects, but a period of marked change to one of his colleagues concerned with other aspects. The eighteenth century is, for example, generally and properly thought of as a static period, but a century beginning with Locke and ending with Kant does not look static to a philosopher, nor one beginning with Purcell and ending with Haydn to a musicologist. For a political or economic historian, or for a historian of the history of ideas, or for a sociologist, the nineteenth century is a century of change, movement and conflict. To the historian of British foreign policy, on the other hand, it is, until near its end, a rather static period. The problems that confronted Castlereagh and Canning continued in large measure to confront their successors.

The problems arising out of the defeat of Napoleon and the Vienna Settlement did not vanish from the European scene until the defeat of France in the Franco-Prussian war. This is neatly illustrated by the titles of two chapters in A. J. P. Taylor's *The Struggle for Mastery in Europe*: 'The Italian War and the Disruption of the Settlement of Vienna' dealing with the unification of Italy, and 'The End of French Primacy, 1870–5' on the Franco-Prussian war. Nor is this true of the Continent alone, for

Britain was concerned with the problem of security from French attack until within sight of the Franco-Prussian War: in the early sixties Palmerston was much agitated by the French conversion of their fleet to 'ironclads', which he regarded, mistakenly it is true, as a deliberate design against this country. In the same way the problems arising out of the Sultan's weakness and the shrinkage of the Turkish Empire persisted right down to the opening of the First World War, from the War of Greek Independence to the Balkan Wars and Sarajevo. As the Sultan's grip weakened, so the subject peoples expressed their determination to achieve national states with greater vigour and success. But nationalism itself goes back to the beginning of the century and has its roots in the French Revolution. It was unseen or ignored by the Congress of Vienna, but within a generation of the Congress it made itself manifest at opposite ends of Europe, in Greece and Belgium. Nor did it affect only Europe, but appeared as far away as Persia and Japan by the end of the century.

Historians would, however, probably agree that there are certain problems posing themselves by the end of the century that are new, even if they are, in one sense, only old problems in a new guise. The threat to Britain from the German navy is new, though that navy itself is no more than a substitute for the French navy. In the same way the Russian threat to China is new, though, as a threat at the same time to the British Empire, it is a threat very similar to that made by the French in India in the eighteenth century. These problems also pose themselves in a new setting. First there were many more people. The population of Europe more than doubled over the century and had increased from 266 million in 1850 to 401 million in 1900. Moreover the proportions of the main European Powers had altered strikingly. The populations of France and Germany were very nearly the same in 1850, but by 1900 Germany had almost half as many people again and was still widening the gap. By 1910 France had the smallest population of any of the Powers except Italy, and Italy was fast catching her up. Russia had by far the largest population and was increasing at about the same rate as Germany. The position is well put by A. J. P. Taylor (Chap. XXVI): 'But, while the French compared their future with Germany's, the Germans looked at another curve—Russia's. Where most of Europe felt over-shadowed by Germany, she saw the more distant Russian shadow; and many Germans thought of anticipating the Russian danger almost as genuinely as others thought of combining against the weight of Germany.'

This steady rise in population acted as a stimulus to industrial production, which was on the increase from a number of other causes as well: the need to reinvest the profits of manufacture; the constantly growing use of power-driven machines; the drive towards units of production of optimum size in order to take full advantage of economies of scale. This increase received an important additional stimulus from the rise in European prices that began about 1895 and went on with only two slight checks in 1901 and 1907 until the outbreak of war in 1914. The increase, and the rate of increase, were greatest for Germany, Russia and the U.S.A. For example, German steel production increased sixfold between 1890 and 1914, Russian tenfold (though from a very low level), and U.S. over sevenfold, while British production did not quite double. Taking industrial production as a whole the annual rate of increase between 1885 and 1913 was for Germany 4·5 per cent, for Russia 5·7 per cent and for the U.S.A. 5·2 per cent, whereas for Great Britain it was only 2·1 per cent.

More goods imply more buyers. Naturally manufacturers looked first of all to their home markets. These they were determined if possible to keep for themselves. In the first half of the nineteenth century there had been a drive of some strength towards free trade; after the end of the American Civil War this was reversed. In 1864 a high tariff was introduced in the U.S.A. as an emergency war measure, but when the war was over the preservation of the home market by a high tariff became the foundation of national policy. After the presidential election of 1889, in which trade policy was an important issue, protection was enshrined in the McKinley Tariff of 1890. After great progress had been made in freeing trade under Napoleon III France returned to limited protection in 1870. Pressure for greater protection increased as a result of the depression in the eighties, and in 1892 the Méline Tariff marked a return to full protection. In Germany the course of events was somewhat similar. A moderate tariff was imposed in 1879. In 1892 Caprivi lowered duties in the interests of the German export trade, but the policy was unpopular, and in 1902 tariffs were again raised, with exemption for raw materials not produced in Germany. After the Russo-Turkish War of 1877–8 Russian duties on imported goods were increased by a third, mainly in order to raise more revenue. From that date onwards protectionist sentiment grew, and in 1891 Witte constructed a tariff with the clear aim of making Russia a self-sufficient economic empire. How much protection contributed to international tension at the beginning of the twentieth century is a matter of controversy. But it is a fact that there was no major European war between 1815 and 1854, a period of steady freeing of trade. On the other hand the free trade current still flowed strongly between 1854 and 1870, when there were such considerable wars as the Italian War of 1859, the Austro-Prussian War of 1866 and the Franco-Prussian War of 1870.

Tariffs protected the home market, but they could not ensure that the home market was large enough to absorb all the goods produced. In fact by 1900 the home markets of Germany and the U.S.A. were not large enough: both countries had become exporters. This led to more international trade, more competition and a search for new markets. As there were few 'empty areas' left in the world this search took the form of a drive to gain exclusive control of a particular area and to establish this as a recognised 'sphere of influence' of the Power concerned. This was most obvious in China.

Increased production and sale led to the continuous creation of capital. Much of this was ploughed back into industry, but much was available for fresh investment, a good deal of it overseas. The export of capital became as important as the export of goods. The greater part of this was privately invested by private companies and banks. But much was provided too by governments directly or indirectly. Striking examples of direct loans are the series of French loans to Russia from 1888 to 1890, the Russian loan to China in 1895 and the Anglo-German loan to China in 1896.

Banks like the Banque de l'Indo-Chine and the Russo-Chinese Bank were founded to promote trade overseas. The Deutsche Asiatische Bank was founded expressly to push German trade in Asiatic Turkey and more particularly to provide capital for constructing the Berlin-Baghdad railway. The normal policy of the British government, as D. C. M. Platt has conclusively shown in his *Finance, Trade and Politics in British Foreign Policy, 1815-1914*, was non-interventionist and devoted solely to preserving 'the open door' for all trade. But where it thought the country's vital interests were at stake even the British government was prepared to take direct action. It not only promoted the Imperial Bank of Persia, clean contrary to its usual practice, but recommended it for the grant of a Royal Charter for providing capital for the construction of railways in Persia and so developing her trade and preventing her being wholly absorbed by Russia.

Railways were in fact, in this period, a matter of great concern to the Powers. They were of course not new, but they were a new factor in international politics. The part played by railways in developing, for example, Canada and the U.S.A. is well known. But Canada and the U.S.A. do not stand alone. In the nineteenth century the railway played the part that had always before been played by the road, a fact most happily emphasised by the American word railroad. To open up wide open spaces it was necessary to build a railroad. The U.S.A. provided the necessary capital for this itself. To build the Trans-Siberian Railway Russia could not, and had to borrow huge sums from France. To build railways in Turkey, Persia, China and South America international capital was needed on a grand scale. To provide some of it international consortia came into being, but there was a strong tendency for individual Powers to finance a particular railway with the double object of controlling the trade and the political relations of the area concerned: e.g. Asiatic Turkey through the Baghdad Railway, Manchuria through the Chinese Eastern Railway, the Yangtze basin through the Shanghai-Nanking railway and the Chinese province of Yunnan through a French railway pushed up from Indo-China over the frontier to Lungchow.

Oil was a new item on the international agenda and it was there because of its possible use as a fuel for ships. In 1898 the Admiralty had set up a committee to consider supplies of fuel-oil. In 1903 a German, Dr. Diesel, had invented an engine burning crude oil that was suitable for ships. By 1914 four per cent of world merchant shipping was using oil. But 'the internal combustion-engine and oil fuel' were, as Herbert Heaton wittily puts it in his *Economic History of Europe* (Harper and Row, 1936), 'clouds bigger than a man's hand on the horizon, but few could see them through the coal dust'. Nevertheless among the few were Sir John ('Jackie') Fisher who became First Sea Lord in 1904 and who was an enthusiast for oil, and Winston Churchill, who became First Lord of the Admiralty in 1911. Churchill sent out a committee of experts to Persia in 1913, and its report led to the government's buying a controlling interest in the Anglo-Persian Oil Company.

Oil was needed for the navy. From 1900 Germany began to build up its navy in competition with Great Britain. As A. J. P. Taylor remarks, 'Navies are more expensive than armies.' So the navy bills helped to push up the sums spent on armaments from 1900 onwards. This of course applied with the greatest force to Britain and Germany, but between 1890 and 1914 expenditure on all armaments rose steadily: British expenditure more than doubled, Austrian and Russian roughly trebled, German almost quadrupled, and even French increased by half. The percentages of national income spent were: British 3.4, German 4.6, French 4.8, Austrian 6.1, and Russian 6.3. (For the full figures see A. J. P. Taylor, pp. xxviii–xxix.) The interpretation of these figures is not quite simple, but it is clear that the quantity of armaments was increasing, and that they were becoming more expensive, which meant that the strain was greatest on the Powers whose economies were most backward and least capable of raising the necessary finance. This might mean that if war was thought to be inevitable it had better come sooner rather than later for these Powers. How far the piling up of armaments made war inevitable, or even more probable, is again a matter of controversy; but it is an argument that has been strongly urged. (See below, p. 112.)

2 Two new Powers—the U.S.A. and Japan Before the Civil War of 1861–5 the U.S.A. had played little part in international affairs, and for some time afterwards the Americans were absorbed in the problems of reconstruction, in pushing the frontier westwards and in realising the industrial potential developed in the course of the war. But in the nineties the U.S.A. emerged on to the international stage. They vigorously intervened in the frontier dispute between Venezuela and British Guiana (see above, p. 29). With much popular backing they went to war with Spain over Cuba in 1898, and as a result annexed Puerto Rico, Guam and the Philippines from Spain, and turned Cuba into something not far short of an American dependency. In 1899 American and British warships jointly intervened in Samoa. Next year American troops took part in the international expedition to Peking to rescue the European residents from the Boxer rebels. A few years later President Theodore Roosevelt played a leading part in persuading the Russians and Japanese to negotiate a peace to conclude the Russo-Japanese War and acted as host to their delegates, who eventually signed a treaty at Portsmouth, New Hampshire in 1905. He also took a vigorous part in support of the Entente at the Algeciras Conference, for which he earned the gratitude and friendship of Sir Edward Grey.

American diplomacy impinged more directly on Britain in another matter at the turn of the century. As a consequence of their Pacific interests the U.S.A. were determined to construct and control a canal linking the Atlantic and the Pacific. This necessitated a revision of the Clayton-Bulwer Treaty of 1850, which defined the attitude of the two Powers to Central America in view of a possible transoceanic canal. The U.S. government made clear from the start of negotiations with the British government not only its determination to control the canal but its effective control of the Caribbean (see below, p. 67).

After the seventeenth century Japan remained virtually unknown to the outer world until the visit of the American sailor, Commodore Perry, in 1853. For some years after this she was exposed to the intervention of the Powers. But in 1867 she abolished the Shogunate, the quasi-feudal governing body that appeared incapable of standing up to foreigners, and under the guidance of a remarkably clear-sighted and able oligarchy, the Genro, began the process of modernising her economic, political and military structure. By the end of the century she was in a position to intervene decisively in the affairs of the Far East.

These offered her a remarkable opportunity. China like Turkey was sick. The feebleness, incompetence and corruption of her government were glaringly revealed by the Taiping Rebellion, which grew out of a 'welter of local uprisings and raids of marauding bandits' and lasted from 1850 to 1864. Worse still, the government showed no desire or capacity to pull itself together and reassert its authority. It stubbornly resisted all change and regarded all outsiders with freezing contempt. This did not matter too much in the middle of the century, as Britain was the only Power much interested in China, and she was concerned to foster her China trade, and on that account to preserve the integrity of China.

But in the last quarter of the century began a process of erosion; from 1890 China became the scene of the bitterest rivalry of the Powers and it looked as if she would totally disintegrate. France, Britain and Russia all infiltrated into the territory of the Chinese Empire. Of these Russia was the most dangerous for China—and for Japan. Korea, a tributary state of China, was of obvious strategic interest to both Russia and Japan. During the eighties there was steady Russian and Japanese infiltration. There were frequent clashes between the Koreans and the Japanese, who were extremely unpopular. Things came to a head in the Tong Hok rebellion in 1894, a rebellion violently hostile to all foreigners. Both China and Japan sent troops to protect their interests. The Korean government put down the rebellion without any outside assistance. Neither China nor Japan withdrew their troops. On the contrary, the Japanese stormed the imperial palace, and set up a puppet Regent, who declared war on China and asked for Japanese help in expelling the Chinese. Japan defeated China hands down, 'liberated' Korea and imposed on China the Treaty of Shimonoseki in 1895. By its terms China was forced to recognise the independence of Korea, to cede to Japan the Liao-

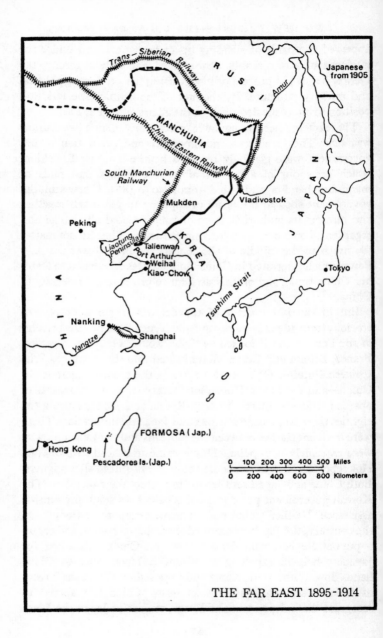

THE FAR EAST 1895-1914

tung peninsula (the Manchurian peninsula to the west of Korea
with Port Arthur at its tip), Formosa and the Pescadores, to pay a
large war indemnity and to open additional ports to foreign trade.

These terms were too much for the Powers. Russia took the
lead in organising a coalition to force Japan to restore the Liao-
tung peninsula to China. This consisted of Russia, France and
Germany, and would have included Britain had the Liberal
Cabinet, at its last gasp, not overruled Rosebery and his Foreign
Secretary, Kimberley, and insisted on staying out. By this
negative act it inadvertently did its Conservative successor a good
turn by leaving the coast clear for a subsequent alliance with
Japan.

In St. Petersburg there was as usual a tug-of-war between
different factions to get and keep control of the Tsar and of
Russian policy. On the whole the Minister of Finance, Witte,
emerged the most successful. He had already promoted the
Trans-Siberian Railway, and his aim now was to postpone a
showdown in the Far East until it was completed (as it was,
though only single-track, in 1905), and in the meantime to secure
a special relationship with China by a mixture of aid and pressure.
To this end he got a French loan for China and in 1896 signed a
fifteen-year pact of mutual defence, whereby each agreed to aid
the other in the event of a Japanese attack on either of them or on
Korea, while China agreed to the construction of a railway across
the Chinese province of Amur in the direction of Vladivostok.
This had a double advantage for Russia: it cut off an awkward
bulge of Chinese territory and so shortened the route of the
Trans-Siberian Railway by hundreds of miles, and it gave her a
useful instrument for the penetration and control of South
Manchuria; but it is worth noting that not a single rail was laid
before the spring of 1900.

This policy was shrewd, but it was wrecked by European
intervention, Chinese weakness and Japanese strength and
determination. In November 1897, using the murder of two
German missionaries as an excuse, Germany demanded and
obtained the 'lease' of Kiao-chow on the Shantung peninsula.
Russian warships thereupon occupied Port Arthur, and the

Russian government demanded from China the 'lease' of Port Arthur and Talienwan, which they obtained in March 1898. France and Britain joined in. The Cabinet was divided on the issue. At first it attempted to stand up to Russia, but it could get no support for its attitude either from the U.S.A. or Japan, so it went into reverse and 'accepted the lease' of Weihai. Salisbury commented, 'It will not be useful, and it will be expensive; but as a matter of pure sentiment, to satisfy the public demand for some territorial or cartographic consolation in China, we shall have to do it.'

Again in 1900, when the Boxer rebellion engulfed all north China and threatened the lives of the European community in Peking, the Powers intervened, this time with the Kaiser as an almost hysterical advocate of violent action. He despatched the German contingent of the international force for the relief of Peking with the words: 'You must know, my men, that you are about to meet a crafty, well-armed, cruel foe! Meet him and beat him! Give no quarter! Take no prisoners! Kill him when he falls into your hands! Even as a thousand years ago, the Huns under their King Attila made such a name for themselves as still resounds in terror through legend and fable, so may the name of German resound through Chinese history a thousand years from now.' In Russia the war party got the upper hand and Russian troops marched into Manchuria. Japan, appealed to by Britain and Russia to send troops at once, was cool, and would send none till she had extracted a promise from the British to pay for the expedition.

These events made it crystal clear in Tokyo that Russian policy in the Far East was not only aggressive but unstable. There seemed to be two possible courses of action: to do a deal with Russia or to come to an agreement with Britain, the one Power that had a fleet capable of keeping the ships of all the other Powers away from the China Sea while Japan settled with Russia. The debate on this question went on throughout the year 1901, and it was only in December that a decision was reached to try for an alliance with Britain. The negotiations were successful and a treaty was signed in January 1902 (see Chapter III).

3 The new Germany Japan had clearly emerged as a new Power and during the last twenty years of the nineteenth century played an increasingly important part on the international stage. But in many respects Germany too was a new Power. The various German kingdoms and principalities had been brought within the German Empire by 1871, and the King of Prussia had become the German Emperor. The process of unifying the German states had been revolutionary and had involved three European wars. But once in existence Germany became a conservative Power. Emperor William I was an intensely conservative man whose influence was wholly on the side of resistance to change. More important, after 1871 Bismarck abjured adventure. At home his policy was devoted to preserving the constitution he had made and his own power; abroad to preserving the balance of power and Germany's position—in his own words quoted above, 'Try to be *à trois* in a world governed by five Powers.' Even Bismarck, however, was pushed into acquiring colonies against his instinct and inclinations

Between 1871 and 1890 Germany's economic strength steadily increased, though her coal production had surpassed that of France even by 1860. Coal production nearly trebled. The production of pig-iron rather more than trebled; that of steel increased almost eight times. The value of German exports rose from £125 million to £170 million. But the really effective expansion of industry and trade occurred after 1890, as the following tables (p. 46) show. By 1914 German coal production nearly equalled British and far exceeded that of the other European countries. Her production of pig-iron had outstripped Britain's; her production of steel was more than twice as large; the other European countries were nowhere. Her chemical and electrical industries led the world. German exports had trebled in value, and competed vigorously with those of Britain: in 1913 they were worth £505 million as against Britain's £653 million. The tonnage of merchant ships had trebled, though it was still only three million tons as compared with the British 11,700,000 tons.

This economic power was translated into military and naval power. The army estimates of the Great Powers increased two-

Coal Production of the Powers, 1870–1914
(in million tons)

	1870	1880	1890	1900	1910	1914
Germany	34	59	89	149	222	277
Austria	8·6	15	26	39	47	47
France	13·3	19·4	26·1	33·4	38·4	40
Britain	112	149	184	228	268	292
Russia	0·75	3·2	6	16·2	24·9	36·2
U.S.A.	10	64·9	143	244	356	455

Pig-iron Production of the Powers, 1870–1914
(in million tons)

	1870	1880	1890	1900	1910	1914
Germany	1·3	2·5	4·1	7·5	9·5	14·7
Austria	0·4	0·5	0·7	1·5	2	2
France	1·2	1·7	2	2·7	4	4·6
Britain	6	7·8	8	9	10	11
Russia	0·4	0·4	0·9	2·9	3	3·6
U.S.A.	1·7	3·9	9·4	14	27	30

Steel Production of the Powers, 1870–1914
(in million tons)

	1870	1880	1890	1900	1910	1914
Germany	0·3	0·7	2·3	6·7	13·8	14
Austria	··	··	0·5	1·2	2·2	2·7
France	0·3	0·4	0·7	1·6	3·4	3·5
Britain	0·7	1·3	3·6	5·0	5·9	6·5
Russia	··	··	0·4	1·5	3·5	4·1
U.S.A.	··	1·3	4·3	10	26	32

Figures from A. J. P. Taylor

and-a-half times between 1890 and 1914, and the navy estimates almost quadrupled, with the really big increase coming between 1900 and 1910. But even more important than the money spent on the services were the crucial strategic decisions of the nineties.

In 1892 General Schlieffen became chief of the German general staff. Like his predecessors he accepted a war on two fronts as the basis of his planning. But unlike them he came to the conclusion that although Russia was weaker than France it would be impossible to deal Russia a knock-out blow owing to her sheer size: bringing the Russian armies to battle would not necessarily produce a decision while the German army in the west contained the French. But in Schlieffen's opinion it would be possible to knock out France provided that Germany had decisive superiority on the western front. The resources of German manpower and production and the technical efficiency of the German high command gave grounds for thinking that this possibility could be realised. Accordingly in November 1892 the Chancellor introduced a new army law providing for the larger army Schlieffen's strategy demanded, which the Reichstag passed the following year. From that time on the Schlieffen plan was the basis of German strategy. This entailed a most important military and political consequence: a Balkan war that involved Austria-Hungary and Russia could not be localised, for Germany was bound to Austria by the Dual Alliance; but if she found herself forced to come to the help of Austria to fend off a Russian attack, she could not deal with Russia until she had first dealt with France.

In 1897 the decision was taken to build a German high seas fleet to replace the existing modest home fleet. This was very largely the personal decision of William II and the chief of the naval staff, Admiral Tirpitz. William's psychology was not simple, and there was more than one motive behind his desire for a big navy, but his attitude was revealed in words uttered in September 1898: 'Our future lies on the water'; and in those he wrote to Bülow at the beginning of the South African War: 'I am not in a position to go beyond the strictest neutrality, and I must first get for myself a fleet. In twenty years' time when the fleet is ready I can use another language.' Tirpitz was a sailor with a passion for his career and a professional's determination that his fleet should be the finest at sea. The Navy Law of 1898 put forward a programme of naval construction designed to cover the period 1898–1903, which included seven battleships and two large cruisers. This was amplified by the Law of 1900, which doubled the number of battleships and increased their size, and set out a timetable of three ships a year to be constructed over the whole of the period 1900–16. The estimated cost was £80 million on ships and £13 million on harbours and docks. Later, in 1906, it was decided to widen the Kiel Canal connecting the Baltic and the

North Sea, originally completed in 1895, so that it could take the new and much larger battleships. The decision to create a German high seas fleet was a fateful one. For, as Balfour remarked, Germany without a fleet was still the strongest Power in Europe, whereas Britain without a fleet was nothing.

Fateful too was the fall of Bismarck in 1890. Bismarck was a great man, and never greater than in his recognition of the limits within which German power could most effectively operate. His successors were little men. William II was not without intelligence, but he was bombastic, unstable and vain; he altogether lacked the largeness of vision, tenacity of purpose and patience that mark the statesman. Caprivi was honest and an excellent administrator but no more. Hohenlohe was an elderly, tired cynic. Bülow was a clever diplomat and a brilliant speaker, but he had no guiding principles and was untrustworthy; it has been well said of him that he was a good tactician but no strategist. Holstein, a foreign office official who acquired much influence on policy after 1890, was morbidly secretive and suspicious; worse still, he had a fixed idea that Germany had nothing to fear from Russia, as it was impossible for Russia to find an ally: Britain was out of the question as Russia would not abandon her expansion in central Asia, and France useless as she could not help Russia in the Straits.

4 New alignment On 17 March 1890 Russia proposed the renewal of the Reinsurance Treaty of 1887 for six years with the possibility of its becoming permanent. Too late. Bismarck had already resigned, and his successors, Caprivi as Chancellor and Marschall as Foreign Minister, were set on a new course of friendship with Britain, which they thought could hardly be squared with friendship with Russia. Advised by Holstein, they felt it safe not to renew the treaty, as they had nothing to fear from Russia. Could France make use of this opportunity to break out of her isolation? Would Russia accept France as a partner instead of Germany? Tsar Alexander III was an intensely conservative man with a proper monarchical contempt for republicanism, but continuous friction with Britain over the Straits and in Asia made an ally very desirable.

Sentiment apart, the main difficulty was that each Power wanted something different. France wanted to secure precise guarantees of aid in the event of war with Germany and to avoid any commitment in the event of an Austro-Russian war; Russia wanted to pin the French down to support against Austria-Hungary, but otherwise to agree to a vague entente, not to sign an alliance. But by the summer of 1891 the Russian government, alarmed by what it imagined to be a grand coalition of the Powers against both Russia and France in the Mediterranean, had made up its mind to negotiate. Agreement was quickly reached on the basis that the two Powers would 'concert their measures on all questions that might threaten peace', and, in case of a danger of aggression, would 'agree on measures whose immediate and simultaneous adoption would be forced on the two Powers by the realisation of that eventuality'. Vague enough, and a victory for Russian policy. But as Ribot remarked, 'The tree is planted.'

Next year it bore fruit in a Military Convention signed on 18 August 1892. Its terms were as follows. If the Triple Alliance, or *one* of its members, mobilised, France and Russia would immediately and simultaneously mobilise and move their forces as near to the frontiers as possible. If France was attacked by Germany, or by Italy backed by Germany, Russia would use all her forces to attack Germany; if Russia was attacked by Germany, or by Austria-Hungary backed by Germany, France would use all her forces to attack Germany. Signature, however, required ratification before the convention became a reality. Tsar Alexander III long delayed his approval, while he hinted to the Kaiser at a rapprochement. The only response he got was the opening of a German tariff war on Russia. So at last he decided for France. An exchange of letters dated 27 December 1893 and 4 January 1894 ratified the convention. The alliance was in being, though it was to be kept absolutely secret.

The fact of the convention being signed was soon known, even though its terms remained absolutely secret. What was its significance? The German historian Schnabel writes: 'Germany's two neighbours in east and west ... had come together: the war on two fronts was from this moment a datum of any future conflict.' For Renouvin the crucial fact is that 'France emerges from the isolation in which Bismarck's policy had kept her'. Nicholas Mansergh thinks that the alliance was more an insurance against German ambitions than anything else. A. J. P. Taylor writes: 'Its serious intention, so far as it had one, was to keep Germany neutral while the two partners pursued their several objects elsewhere. All the same, it was a weapon loaded only against Germany, whatever the reservations of the two partners.' On the other hand Halévy thought that 'if in its inception the Franco-Russian Alliance was aimed at Germany, it had possessed from the outset another aspect, hostility towards Great Britain'.

For Russia the alliance was clear gain. The Tsar already knew that in the event of a Russian attack on Austria-Hungary Germany was pledged to come to her help, for Bismarck had been forced to reveal to him the terms of the Austro-German Alliance of 1879 in order to bring off the Reinsurance Treaty. So the Tsar held the initiative. If Austria-Hungary was provoked into attacking Russia, Germany had an excuse for inaction and France was Russia's automatic ally; if, on the other hand, it suited Russia to attack first, Germany would be forced to help Austria-Hungary and this would in all probability bring France in on Russia's side. In fact it would have brought France in with absolute certainty, because the Schlieffen Plan, as we have seen, entailed an attack on France; but this was not known to the Tsar; he could only make an intelligent guess. On top of this the alliance was bound to strengthen Russia's position in relation to Britain, for, in the event of a Russian seizure of the Straits, the French fleet in the Mediterranean could prevent the British fleet interfering, as the British Admiralty recognised. Furthermore it might well stop the British Far Eastern fleet interfering with Russian expansion in the China Sea. It seems, therefore, as if Halévy's comment may be misleading. It is certainly true that from the Russian point of view the alliance possessed another aspect, but one that took Britain into account rather than showing hostility towards her. The alliance was only hostile to Britain in the sense that it strengthened the Russian hand in dealings with her in both the Near and the Far East.

There can be no doubt that Renouvin is right in emphasising

France's emergence from isolation. The alliance clearly rescued France from isolation, and this was very welcome at a time when relations with Britain were so bad. On the other hand the alliance, from the French point of view, was aimed at Germany, and not Britain, and in that point its value for France is more doubtful. There was no longer any danger of a preventive war by Germany on France; the danger was of an attack on France to prevent Germany having to fight a war on two fronts. This danger to France was surely increased by the knowledge that France and Russia were now allies, whatever the exact terms of the alliance. Furthermore there was a considerable risk of France being dragged into war over the Balkans. Though it was not perhaps likely that Russia would attack Austria-Hungary directly, or vice versa, it must be remembered that the time when the Franco-Russian Alliance was made was one of bad relations between Russia and Austria-Hungary before the understanding of 1897 that put the Balkan Question on ice for a decade. Given the explosive situation in the Balkans, the instability of both Austrian and Russian policy and the resources of diplomacy in manoeuvring a state into committing an act of aggression (Cavour's provocation of Austria in 1859 is not to be forgotten), it is no wonder that France was so anxious to avoid a clause pledging her to help Russia if she was attacked by Austria-Hungary.

Why then did the French government take the initiative for an alliance and why was it so keen to conclude it? Not for Alsace-Lorraine. The evidence is that feeling about the lost provinces had died down; while no doubt all Frenchmen looked forward to their eventual recovery, few but extremists contemplated an aggressive war to recover them at this moment. In a way, however, it was Alsace-Lorraine that was at the bottom of French policy. France was at odds with Italy over Tunis and Tripoli, and with Britain in various parts of Africa and in S.E. Asia. Her most natural ally against Italy was Austria-Hungary, but Austria-Hungary could hardly turn against Italy, the third partner in the Triple Alliance, without breaking up the alliance and so incurring German wrath and, perhaps, forfeiting her support. Germany was France's most natural ally against Britain, and over the last decade Germany had been very ready to blackmail Britain when she needed German support over Egypt and West Africa. But extracting advantage from the exposed British position in Africa was one thing, continuous and reliable friendship with France another: so long as Germany retained Alsace-Lorraine this was impossible. If France was to escape from isolation it could only be through alliance with Russia. Isolation was humiliating and perhaps felt more dangerous than it was; prestige, dreams of glory and illusory safety beckoned.

How would the alliance affect Britain? Formally it did not in any way alter her relationship to the Powers, for she was not in alliance with any of them. But in practice it would, in all probability, affect the balance of power in international affairs and so necessitate some adjustment of British policy. The problem was to assess exactly to what degree the balance was affected and exactly what regulatory action was called for. The British reaction is the theme of the next chapter.

Chapter III

The end of the 'free hand'

1 An Anglo–German alliance? The end of the nineteenth century was a period of great unease, or what G. M. Young in his *Victorian England*, (O.U.P. 1936) goes so far as to call 'Titanic chaos'. 'We may easily censure the diplomacy of the Imperialist age too harshly,' he writes (pp. 180–1), 'if we forget in what Titanic chaos it was involved. A still increasing population supported increasingly on foreign food; an industrial and commercial lead that was steadily lessening; the longest of frontiers guarded by the smallest of armies [though the service vote rose from £31 million in 1890 to £47 million in 1899]; communications encircling the world, but threaded on coaling stations that a venturesome squadron might annihilate in an afternoon; Australians snarling at the German flag in the Pacific; Newfoundland threatening to join the United States; English and Dutch eyeing one another for the mastery of South Africa; West Africa undelimited; China collapsing; Russia in search of an open sea; markets closing or opening as new tariffs are set up or spheres of influence staked out; what policy, one may ask, was possible in such a world, except the seeming no-policy of maintaining the frail Concert of Europe, of easing all contacts, with Germany in Africa, with France on the Mekong; and making the Fleet invincible at all costs? Isolation, splendid or not, was forced on the England of Rosebery and Salisbury as it had been chosen by the England of Canning and Palmerston.'

Salisbury remained true to this 'seeming no-policy' until his death, but there were a number of ministers in his last government who were increasingly uneasy at the exposed position of Britain in the world and were beginning to think that safety lay not in isolation but in an alliance with one of the Powers. Among them were Arthur Balfour, Salisbury's nephew, who deputised for him when he was away ill, and who knew more about Europe than most other members of the Cabinet and was perturbed by the alteration in the balance of power produced by the Franco-Russian Alliance; Lansdowne, the Secretary of State for War, who succeeded Salisbury at the Foreign Office in 1900; and Hamilton, the Secretary of State for India, much concerned at the Russian threat to India through Persia and Afghanistan. Above all there was Joseph Chamberlain, the most colourful figure in the government, whose reputation had been made in local government and as a radical reformer, but who had surprised everyone by going to the Colonial Office when Salisbury had formed his government in 1895. Chamberlain was, in his biographer's words, 'a man of principle, rather than principles; more concerned with ends than with means; dedicated to serving the nation and seeing political parties not as causes in themselves but rather as instruments to get things done' (Julian Amery, *The Life of Joseph Chamberlain*, Macmillan, 1969, vol. 6, p. 994). Other observers saw him with a rather different eye: Paul Cambon wrote, 'Mr. Chamberlain has no political principles. He lives in the present and changes his opinions with incredible ease. . . . He has a very accurate sense of what public opinion wants and follows its fluctuations while having the air of guiding them—hence his popularity'; while as long ago as 1886 Gladstone had warned Bryce that 'Chamberlain was a most dangerous man, reckless, ambitious, unscrupulous, and that the country would suffer from him'.

What was there in the situation that had produced this shift of opinion among leading politicians? To the contemporary eye there was no dramatic change in the position of Britain. Her economic power, it is true, was steadily weakening in relation to Germany and the U.S.A., but slowly and almost imperceptibly; the most visible challenge on the economic horizon was Russia's threat to the China trade. At home the national income was still increasing and the standard of living rising steadily; political stability went hand-in-hand with economic progress. Abroad the Empire was at its greatest extent and the control of the mother country was still assured. British 'naval preponderance was greater than ever in our history': the French navy was greatly inferior in material and men; the Russian navy, the third largest in the world, was notoriously inefficient; the German existed as yet only on paper; the Japanese was small and untried, as was that of the U.S.A.; and in any event they were the fleets of friendly Powers with whom Britain had no conflicting interests.

By 1897, however, Britain was isolated in a far more literal sense than she had been for many years. Relations with France and Russia were as bad as at any time in the last quarter of a century: there was constant friction with France in Africa, and to the threat to India from Central Asia were added the Russian drive into Manchuria and North China and the consequent threat to the China trade, that had by this time become so important to the British economy. Colonial rivalry with Germany in Africa and the Far East had impaired Anglo-German relations. Salisbury's change of policy in regard to the Straits and refusal to guarantee the defence of Constantinople had decided Austria-Hungary to sever the link forged by the Mediterranean Agreements of the eighties. The British and Austrian decisions automatically loosened the bonds between Britain and Italy, for Britain now had no need of Italian co-operation in her policy towards Russia over the Straits, and had consistently refused to guarantee Italy against a French attack; nor was an agreement to preserve peace in the Mediterranean, without Austrian participation, of much attraction or value to either Power.

Between the spring of 1898 and the end of 1901 a determined effort was made to alter this situation: under pressure from Chamberlain the government tried not merely to draw closer to Germany but to bring about an alliance between the two Powers. The rapprochement took shape in agreements about the Portuguese colonies in Africa and about China. By the Anglo-German Agreement (1898) the two Powers agreed to guarantee a joint loan to Portugal, with various parts of the Portuguese colonies as security in case of default, and in a secret convention provided for the partition of the colonies should it 'unfortunately not be found possible to maintain the integrity of the African possessions of Portugal south of the Equator'. The Boxer Rebellion in China led to an agreement between Britain and Germany to restrain territorial aggression in China and to guarantee the principle of the 'open door' in Chinese trade, an agreement known to the British as The Anglo-German China Agreement (1900) and to the Germans as the Yangtze Agreement. This difference of name symbolises the ambiguity of the agreement: to the Germans it was an agreement to prevent the British monopolising the trade of the Yangtze valley and so to open it to German economic penetration, to the British an agreement guaranteeing various spheres of influence in China and so barring North China to Russian advance. It is not surprising that it never became of any practical importance.

It did not lead, as the China committee of the Cabinet had hoped, to a general Anglo-German agreement on China, still less to an alliance. Repeated attempts were made during this period to bring about an alliance: from March to August 1898; in November 1899, when the Kaiser paid a very popular visit to Queen Victoria at a difficult moment in the South African War; and throughout 1901. All foundered on the same fundamental reef: Germany was not willing to give Britain armed support against Russia in the Far East, or, in Bülow's phrase, 'to pull the chestnuts out of the fire' in China, unless Britain was willing in return to join the Triple Alliance and assume the full responsibilities of an ally, in Europe as well as in Asia; put the other way round, Britain was not willing to join the Triple Alliance and run the risk of being dragged into a war with France for the sake of German backing in the Far East.

The arguments against an alliance had certainly been strengthened by events since the beginning of 1898. The British navy had effectively deterred France from going to war after Fashoda (see above, p. 28), and the attempt at a European coalition against Britain to take advantage of her involvement in the South

African War had come to nothing. Salisbury summed the matter up in a memorandum written in May 1901. In the first place, he argued, 'The liability of having to defend the German and Austrian frontiers against Russia is heavier than that of *having to defend the British Isles against France*.' So an alliance with Germany would be a bad bargain. Nor is it necessary. Allies would not have saved Britain from Napoleon had he commanded the Channel. The Powers, on the other hand, have shown themselves incapable of allying with one another to take advantage of British 'isolation'. So 'it would hardly be wise to incur novel and most onerous obligations, in order to guard against *a danger in whose existence we have no historical reason for believing*.'

'But ... these are not by any means the weightiest objections that can be urged against it. The fatal circumstance is that *neither we nor the Germans are competent to make the suggested promises*.' For in a parliamentary state no government is able to bind its successor, and this would apply as much to Germany as to Britain, except that the German parliament would probably pay more attention to the wish of its executive than would the British Parliament. On the other hand 'a *promise of defensive alliance with England would excite bitter murmurs in every rank of German society*', if recent manifestations of German opinion were to be trusted.

Salisbury's instinct was not at fault. The British Press, which had been violently anti-French at the time of Fashoda, had likewise been violently nationalistic and anti-foreign during the South African War; and despite the moral effect of the Kaiser's visit to Queen Victoria in 1899 its reaction to Chamberlain's speech at Leicester on 30 November, in which he proposed an Anglo-Saxon-Teutonic alliance, was outspokenly hostile. This attitude hardened into one of rigid anti-Germanism. Not long after Salisbury's memorandum occurred an episode that produced effects out of all proportion to its size. In a speech at Edinburgh in October 1901 Chamberlain defended a policy of severer repression that the government might have to adopt against the Boer guerillas, and remarked that it had precedents for such a policy 'in the action of those nations who now criticise our "barbarity"' and "cruelty", but whose example in Poland, in the Caucasus, in Algeria, in Tongking, in Borneo, in the Franco-German war—whose example we have never even approached'. This did not rouse much excitement in France or Russia, but in Germany it led to such an outcry that Bülow felt it necessary to administer a rebuke to Chamberlain in the Reichstag. 'This episode', in Halévy's words, 'produced a strange effect on British opinion. Undercurrents of mistrust which the German policy had aroused, but which, hitherto, had been submerged by incompatible or contradictory sentiments, rose suddenly to the surface.' (Elie Halévy, *A History of the English People in the Nineteenth Century*, Benn, revised edition 1951, vol 5, p. 123.) Emotions emerged from the subconscious and embodied themselves in thoughts, in words, in print.

2 Extra-European agreements: Japan and the U.S.A.

Neither the failure of the Anglo-German negotiations nor Salisbury's memorandum deflected the advocates of an alliance from their policy. Salisbury's powers were obviously failing during his last two years in office, and it was perhaps to be expected that his colleagues should think his ideas as outworn as his physique; it was natural that men of a younger generation should react with the vigour of maturity to the ideas of a man born as long ago as 1830—in the year Palmerston became Foreign Secretary and before the passage of the Great Reform Bill.

The man who succeeded Salisbury as Foreign Secretary in 1900 was, like him, an aristocrat. Henry Charles Keith Petty-Fitzmaurice, 5th Marquis of Lansdowne, was born in 1845. He succeeded to the title at the age of twenty-one. Between the ages of thirty-eight and forty-nine he was in succession Governor-General of Canada and Viceroy of India. In 1895, when he was fifty, he became Secretary of State for War in Salisbury's government. By the time he became Foreign Secretary in 1900 he was therefore a highly experienced administrator, but he had comparatively little experience of Parliament and none of the House of Commons. He was a man of great integrity, reserved and cool, intelligent but rather unimaginative. He paid more attention to the judgement of his expert advisers than did Salisbury, who had an ingrained belief that experts were as likely to be wrong as right. This was the man who was to set a 'new course' for British foreign policy.

The situation that confronted him in the Far East when he took up office was a disagreeable one for Britain. Ever since her defeat at the hands of Japan in 1894-5 China had been under constant pressure from the Powers. A coalition of Russia, Germany and France had forced Japan to give back her conquests of the Liao-tung peninsula and Port Arthur to China, but this apparent generosity to China concealed their own designs. China gave Russia a concession to build a branch railway line from the Trans-Siberian Railway across Manchuria to Vladivostok. In 1898 Russia occupied Port Arthur and in 1900, in the chaos that reigned in North China during and after the Boxer Rebellion, extended her occupation to the whole of Manchuria. The other Powers were not backward in joining in the scramble for Chinese territory; they acquired what were euphemistically called 'leases' of various ports.

Lansdowne was much concerned about the situation but was cautious about a possible alliance with Japan to protect mutual interests, particularly so long as the negotiations with Germany were in progress. Nevertheless before the ministers dispersed for their holidays in the summer of 1901 he had had several meetings with the Japanese Minister, Hayashi, and had decided that matters had reached a point where he should inform the Cabinet. After the meeting Salisbury reported to the King that negotiations were in progress and would be pursued.

When Lansdowne returned from Ireland in October he had before him two important departmental memoranda: one drawn up by his own officials, and one produced by Selborne, the First Lord of the Admiralty. The Foreign Office memorandum bore the heading, 'Anglo-Japanese Agreement: reasons why one is desirable and why Germany should not be included'. It noted that Japan had proposed that the Powers should agree to see that the most-favoured nation principles should be applied to all grants of territory in China; that Japan was anxious to check Russian expansion in Manchuria short of going to war; and that she was more determined to keep Russia out of Korea and might value British help in protecting Japanese security and interests there. It went on to ask whether Britain should give any help. A Russian occupation of Korea would pose such a threat to British interests in China that Britain would be bound to resist it, and it was therefore best to give Japan such practical help as she could; this must take the form of financial and naval aid. Germany should not be included in an alliance because she would never risk offending Russia for the sake of Japanese interests in Korea.

Selborne also strongly supported an alliance from the naval angle. He began by stating that the two-Power Standard was no longer operable against France and Russia owing to the dispersal of the British fleet. He then remarked (somewhat parenthetically) that if the U.S.A. chose to build up their fleet it would, together with the fleet of a second Power, be superior to that of Britain. If war should break out with France it would be fought in the Channel and the Mediterranean, and therefore the fleet would have to be concentrated in home waters; but this made it impossible to maintain naval supremacy in the Caribbean and the Far East as well. On the other hand it was essential to hold Hong Kong and to protect our China trade. This pointed to an ally in the Far East. On its own the British fleet would be inferior to the combined French and Russian fleets (assuming that they could effect a junction) in a ratio of 4 to 9 in battleships and 16 to 20 in cruisers. But with the Japanese fleet it would have a superiority of 11 to 9 in battleships and a preponderance in cruisers.

Whether Lansdowne had made up his mind to go for a Japanese alliance when he returned from Ireland is uncertain. If he had, these memoranda would have strengthened his resolve; if he had not, they must have helped him come to a decision. In fact at this juncture British and Japanese policies were almost alike: to explore simultaneously the possibility of an understanding with Russia and, if that were fruitless, an alliance with the most suitable partner, Japan in the one case and Britain in the other.

In the middle of October Lansdowne saw Hayashi, hoping to get from him concrete proposals for an alliance. His hope was disappointed. On the strength of this interview and of the news that Ito, a senior Japanese politician, was visiting Paris and St. Petersburg, Lansdowne prepared two memoranda for the Cabinet: a draft treaty of alliance with Japan and a draft proposal for ending Anglo-Russian friction, especially in Persia and the Far East. It is clear in a general way that Lansdowne wanted to ease Britain's international position. What is not clear is how far he had any genuine belief in the approach to Russia or made it in the near-certainty of rebuff, with a view to the effect that such a rebuff would have on his colleagues. Perhaps this is to put things too clearly: at this moment Lansdowne did not know the mind of the Russians or of the Japanese or even his own. A Russian answer, one way or the other, might help to clarify at least two of these. On 28 October the Cabinet approved the approach to Russia. Lansdowne did not have to wait long for his answer. By 2 November Russia rejected the British approach. The ground was cleared for an alliance with Japan.

The Cabinet met and took the decision on 5 November. Next day Lansdowne submitted his draft treaty to Hayashi. For a month there was a loud silence. This seemed ominous to Lansdowne. Indeed it was, for what was happening in Tokyo was what had already happened in London and in Lansdowne's own mind—a great debate on the merits of an alliance. Powerful members of the Genro were in favour of an alliance with Britain, but what was eventually decisive was that Ito could get nothing satisfactory out of the Russians. On 7 December the Genro council decided for an alliance with Britain. On 12 December Hayashi brought the Japanese draft to Lansdowne. The treaty was signed on 30 January 1902.

In the preamble to the treaty the two Powers state that they are 'actuated solely by a desire to maintain the *status quo* and general peace in the Far East' and especially to maintain 'the independence and territorial integrity' of China, Korea and the 'open door'. They then declare their special interests in China and Korea, and 'recognise that it will be admissible for either of them to safeguard those interests if threatened either by the aggressive action of any other Power, or by disturbance arising in China or

Korea, and necessitating the intervention of either of the High Contracting Parties for the protection of the lives or property of their subjects'. In the event of either Power being involved in war with one other Power, the other will preserve strict neutrality; in the event of war with two Powers one will aid the other and 'will conduct the war in common and make peace in mutual agreement with it'. The alliance was to run for five years.

During the negotiations for the alliance the Cabinet made some effort to extend it to cover south-east Asia and India, but Japan was adamant in refusing to consider this and the Cabinet had to submit. Lansdowne was content to do so, as he believed that the alliance in the form in which it was signed gave valuable protection to British interests.

What were these interests? First was the China trade, which meant particularly trade up the Yangtze valley. This was threatened more by the disintegration of China itself than by specific inroads by the Russians, the Germans or the French. But it is fair to say that the greatest threat to Chinese integrity came from Russia, so that anything that checked Russian aggression and the Russian absorption of China indirectly protected British trade. Support for Japan in Korea might well keep the Russians out of it and check their progress in Manchuria. But it might well involve war.

Britain's second interest in the Far East was peace. Peace was needed for trade to flourish. War in the Far East at a time when the Admiralty was concentrating British warships in home waters (see below, p. 74) would have been decidedly inconvenient for Britain. Worse, war in the Far East might only too easily spread to Europe. A major war could not but damage British trade the world over, and there was no telling what the consequences might be for Britain, Europe and the world.

It was not easy to forecast whether the alliance would make for peace in the Far East, for this depended on its effect on policy in Russia and Japan; and in neither country was policy stable and predictable. In Russia there was a continuous struggle for control, and at any time a party favourable to an understanding with Japan might have gained the ear of the Tsar. Then Russia might well have been content to realise her Far Eastern ambitions by controlling the railways to Vladivostok and Port Arthur, and securing the warm-water port on the Liao-tung peninsula. On the other hand Witte's long-term policy for the development of Siberia involved Russian control of Chinese policy, which was intolerable to both Japan and Britain. Nor was Japanese official opinion unanimous. Before the alliance was concluded there was a great debate; the conclusion of the alliance did not overnight convert those in favour of a rapprochement with Russia. Just as Russia might realise her ambitions in the Far East by agreeing to share control of North China with Japan, so Japan might realise hers by sharing control with Russia. The question is whether the conclusion of the Anglo-Japanese Alliance strengthened the peace party or the war party. On this there is a direct conflict of opinion between the scholars who have most recently considered the matter. (See J. A. S. Grenville, pp. 390–1 and I. H. Nish, *The Anglo-Japanese Alliance*, p. 239.) More light is thrown on the question by a Cabinet memorandum written by Arthur Balfour on 29 December 1903, when events in the Far East were already moving towards war. In this he argues that Britain must fulfil her legal obligations under the alliance, 'in the spirit as in the letter', but that any attempt to base British policy on moral obligations that exceeded the legal obligations would make for war, not for peace.

'The original policy of the Anglo-Japanese Treaty', he writes, 'depended essentially on the theory, openly avowed I think by Japan at the time, that she was a match for Russia alone, but not a match for Russia and another Power in combination.' In other words Japan might find herself involved in a war brought on by Russian aggression, in which Russia had the support of her European ally, France. To guard against this Japan too needed an ally. This she had found in Britain. Balfour then goes on: 'And criticism must develop into condemnation if the policy of the Treaty is so stretched as to imply something like a moral obligation to help Japan whenever she seems likely to be beaten by Russia. Then the Japanese Alliance would become not a guarantee of peace, but the inevitable occasion of war. It would be a standing international danger. For since, by hypothesis, Japan single-handed is not a match for Russia, we should *always* have to go to her assistance in case of hostilities between the two. France in such an event being bound to throw in her lot with Russia, the government at Tokyo would be the arbiters of peace and war for half the civilised world!' Balfour in his capacity as Prime Minister is considering the effects of the alliance on British interests, and concluding that, as strictly interpreted by the British government, it was likely to prevent any war in the Far East between Japan and Russia spreading into an international war. But in the course of his argument he lets slip a judgement of some significance: 'By hypothesis, Japan single-handed is not a match for Russia', but at the same time, 'The original policy of the Anglo-Japanese Treaty depended essentially on the theory, openly avowed I think by Japan at the time, that she was a match for Russia alone.' Britain might expect Japan not to risk war with Russia single-handed; but this was not necessarily the expectation of Japan herself.

War in fact broke out early in 1904, and the speed and completeness of Japan's victory took all the Powers by surprise. Well before the conclusive naval battle of Tsushima in May 1905 and the subsequent peace negotiations Britain had taken the initiative for a renewal of the original alliance before the end of its term. A new treaty was signed in August 1905, to run for ten years. It extended the obligations of the original alliance to include the mutual defence of the territorial rights and interests of the two Powers in Eastern Asia. Specifically this meant the possibility of armed assistance if Korea or India were attacked. Further each ally pledged herself to assist the other if attacked by *one* Power only, not *two* as in the original treaty. This secured Japan against a war of revenge by Russia and gave Britain valuable reassurance against an attack by Russia on the Indian Empire.

The original alliance raises another question of great interest to historians, and especially to historians of British foreign policy: did the alliance end 'splendid isolation' and inaugurate a 'new course'? Lansdowne himself thought it did. He defended the treaty in the House of Lords by arguing that isolation was out of date. 'I do not think', he said, 'that anyone can have watched the recent course of events in different parts of the world without realising that many of the arguments which a generation ago might have been adduced in support of a policy of isolation have ceased to be entitled to the same consideration now. What do we see on all sides?' Ever-increasing armaments, war breaking out with a new suddenness when nations are armed to the teeth. In view of this, 'We must surely feel that that country would indeed be endowed with an extraordinary amount of what I might call self-sufficiency which took upon itself to say that it would accept, without question, without reservation, the doctrine that all foreign alliances were to be avoided as necessarily embarrassing and objectionable.' There were even some opponents of the alliance who were willing to agree that it did indeed end Britain's isolation. Hicks-Beach, for example, one of the few members of the Cabinet who was against the alliance and who was of the opinion that it would never have been concluded had Salisbury still been at the Foreign Office, agreed with Lansdowne on this. So did the leaders of the Liberal opposition, who attacked the alliance as an unnecessary departure from traditional policy.

Most historians have agreed with them. Gooch wrote that the alliance's 'epoch-making character was recognised by friend and foe', and the Austrian historian Pribram that 'The extraordinary significance of the Anglo-Japanese alliance for world politics lay in the fact that with its conclusion England ceased to follow the policy of splendid isolation which had been her course for so many years.' Harold Temperley and Lillian Penson set it in a wider context (p. 521): 'The Treaty was', they write, 'revolutionary, a departure not only from the principles of Salisbury but even from those of Canning, which deprecated increase of obligations by guarantees or alliances. . . . England could not remain friendly to or co-operate with Russia in Europe, if she was bound by an alliance to restrain her aggression in Asia. An alliance, even if confined to a limited sphere, was in the end bound to cause a departure from Salisbury's principles and to inaugurate a new age.' Against this A. J. P. Taylor writes: 'The Alliance did not mark the end of British isolation; rather it confirmed it. Isolation meant aloofness from the European Balance of Power; and this was now more possible than before.' Is this a conflict of substance or merely of verbal definition? The words of Temperley and Penson imply that Salisbury's policy was in essence Canning's, a policy chary of guarantees or alliances, that might in this context usefully be compared with George Washington's policy for the U.S.A. of no 'entangling alliances'. The enunciation of the Monroe Doctrine was made possible by the existence of the British fleet. Did its existence in 1900 make possible the insulation of the Far East from Europe?

Curiously, it was the growth of the U.S. fleet that led to a major settlement with the U.S.A. The Spanish-American War of 1898 had made the U.S.A. aware of the need for a canal connecting the Atlantic and Pacific oceans. But the cutting of a canal implied too a revision of the Clayton-Bulwer Treaty (1850) which gave Britain equal control of any such canal, for the U.S.A. were determined to have sole control. Accordingly in 1899 President McKinley's Secretary of State, Hay, opened negotiations for revision of the treaty. On 12 January the British ambassador in Washington, Sir Julian Pauncefote, sent home Hay's draft convention, which, as is now known, had largely been drawn up by Pauncefote himself. Its terms were: that the right to construct, regulate and manage a canal in Central America was conceded to the U.S.A.; that the canal should remain free and open to all ships, merchant ships and warships alike, 'in time of war as in time of peace'; that it could not be blockaded nor fortifications erected for its defence, though the U.S.A. were given the right of policing it; that other countries be given the right to adhere to the convention.

The negotiations were drawn out, mainly owing to the British insistence on linking the convention to the defining of the U.S.-Canadian frontier in Alaska, and eventually lapsed. But the outbreak of the South African War made the British government anxious to put its relations with the U.S.A. on as good a footing as possible. Negotiations reopened in January 1901, and a draft convention was quickly signed. American opinion was however extremely jingoistic at this time, and the Senate inserted an amendment giving the U.S.A. the right to make such dispositions as might be necessary for the defence of the U.S.A. and for the maintenance of public order. This was unacceptable to the British government.

Lansdowne was clear in his mind that Britain should sign the convention even in its amended form. He judged, rightly, that American opinion was so strong that it would insist on an American-controlled canal, and would, if provoked, force the U.S. government to pass a bill simply abrogating the Clayton-Bulwer Treaty, in which case the U.S.A. would have a completely free hand. He was also convinced, largely on the strength of an Admiralty memorandum, that control of the canal would inevitably lie with the Power controlling the sea approaches to it, and that this Power could only be the U.S.A. Britain was no longer strong enough to control the Caribbean. Above all Lansdowne was convinced of the paramount importance of Anglo-U.S. friendship. For this he was prepared to pay a stiff price, if necessary. But he thought that determination and skilful diplomacy might prevent the Americans going it alone and ignoring the rights and interests of other countries. In this he was proved right. After negotiations that lasted throughout the summer of 1901 he secured the acceptance of two principles: that there should be no change of sovereignty over the area through which the canal passed; and that the freedom of the canal should be confined to those Powers 'which shall agree to observe these rules', thus obliquely ensuring that any other country might be associated with the convention governing the working of the canal.

The treaty, known as the Hay-Pauncefote Treaty, was signed in Washington in November 1901 and ratified by the Senate in December. It put Anglo-American relations on a new footing and opened the way to a period in which good relations between the two countries were taken for granted, so that many people on both sides of the Atlantic came to think of them as 'natural'. It registered the crucial British decision to withdraw from the Caribbean. 'It was,' in Grenville's words, 'perhaps Lansdowne's greatest achievement as Foreign Secretary.'

3 The Entente Cordiale The Anglo-Japanese Treaty and the Hay-Pauncefote Treaty were successes for British diplomacy, but at the time they were signed they were not successes of the first magnitude; their significance lay in the future. Neither of them did anything to improve the British position in relation to Russia, and the Anglo-Japanese Treaty possibly worsened it with the distinct chance of being drawn into a war with Russia over Korea.

Relations with Russia were bad: Macedonia, Persia, Afghanistan and China were areas of conflict, in any one of which war might have broken out in 1902 or 1903. Curzon, the Viceroy of India, who had a grandiose imperial imagination and an almost Renaissance belief in *virtù* and fame, was continually pressing for a forward policy against Russia and for more troops for India. Balfour, Prime Minister since July 1902, was deeply interested in imperial strategy and concerned, perhaps even obsessed, with India. So was the Committee of Imperial Defence, founded in December 1902, largely at Balfour's instigation (see below, p. 73). Furthermore the committee decided in 1903 that there was no threat of invasion of the British Isles, and thus subtly altered the attitude of the politicians to France and to the Franco-Russian Alliance. King Edward VII, who had ascended the throne in January 1901, distrusted the Russians and was consistently in favour of a determined attitude towards them. Lansdowne himself was very conscious of the Russian threat to British interests and was anxious not to put a foot wrong. Both his temperament and the situation of his country, just emerged from a very expensive war that had been a great psychological shock to the country, inclined him towards easing relations with the Powers. In this he found support from the Admiralty too, as it had come to the conclusion that the German fleet was designed solely for war against the British; from this followed a determination to increase the size of the British Navy and to avoid trouble with France and Russia.

Working with Germany proved impossible. Lansdowne had an excellent opportunity when the question of financing the Baghdad Railway arose in the spring of 1903. The Germans could not raise all the capital themselves and were inviting co-operation. Lansdowne, backed by the War Office, was anxious to respond for strategic reasons: he thought the railway would be a valuable

instrument for countering Russian expansion in Persia and that it
would be wise for Britain to contribute to the loan and so have a
say in its management. But public opinion, perhaps, as A. J. P.
Taylor suggests, incited by British financiers, was too strong for
him. Throughout 1902 feeling against Germany ran high, and a
press campaign, backed by Chamberlain, against taking part in
the scheme forced Lansdowne to abandon his policy; he had to be
content with a declaration that Britain would regard a fortified
port on the Persian Gulf as a grave menace to British interests and
one that it would resist at all costs.

But as Bertie, the Assistant Under-Secretary at the Foreign
Office, remarked in the autumn of 1903, 'For us France is more
important than Germany or Russia or any other Power. If we are
certain of France, no one can have designs upon us.' Here
Lansdowne was fortunate. The new French ambassador, Paul
Cambon, had arrived in London to take up his post in December
1898 with instructions to seek a settlement of the various points at
issue between Britain and France. He and Lansdowne made some
progress on minor points of friction such as the Newfoundland
fisheries and the joint frontiers of Siam, Malaya and Indo-China,
but Lansdowne showed no disposition to come to grips with the
key question of Morocco. He was for letting sleeping Moroccan
dogs lie and did his best to avoid the subject altogether. Meanwhile
the French Foreign Minister, Delcassé, had been steadily isolating
Britain in Morocco. He had made certain that Germany did not
regard her vital interests as involved there; he had come to an
agreement with Italy by which France would give Italy a free hand
in Tripoli as soon as the situation was ripe for French annexation
of Morocco; and by the end of 1902 had almost signed a treaty of
partition with Spain to the complete exclusion of Britain.

But events in Morocco and the Far East frustrated his plans and
forced Lansdowne and himself to come to terms. In December
1902 there was a rebellion in Morocco, the rebels got to within
forty miles of Fez and there seemed to be a danger of complete
disintegration. This led to a reversal of French policy: instead of
wanting to liquidate Morocco they now wanted to preserve the
status quo. It also led to a change of attitude in Britain, and

towards the end of the month Lansdowne for the first time expressed to Cambon a desire for an understanding on Morocco. But, as Cambon had already pointed out, an agreement on Morocco meant an agreement on Egypt. Ever since 1882 Britain had been the victim of France's resentment at having withdrawn from Egypt in 1881 and of persistent French hostility that had enabled Germany to blackmail Britain into colonial concessions. It was inconceivable that she would now meekly join hands with the French to patch things up in Morocco unless she got assurances that France now accepted the position in Egypt and would cease from hostile interference. This however was a major stumbling block for Delcassé, for he had what amounted to an obsession with Egypt. Perhaps the necessity for a Moroccan settlement would in the last resort have overcome his distaste for a renunciation of Egypt, but events in the Far East gave him a final push.

The Russians, who had been in occupation of Manchuria since the Boxer rebellion in 1900, were due to begin the evacuation, several times postponed, in April 1903. Instead when the date came they produced fresh demands on China. Strong protests by Britain, the U.S.A. and Japan made Russia withdraw her demands, but not evacuate Manchuria. Japanese patience was almost exhausted, and the risk of war between her and Russia became much more acute. If war broke out, Russia would appeal for French support under the terms of the Franco-Russian Alliance. France would be faced with a choice: either to abandon the alliance or to honour it and find herself at war not only with Japan, but with Japan's ally, Britain. Whichever way she chose she would do herself no good; she would undermine the achievements of French diplomacy since the fall of Bismarck and benefit only Germany. This was decisive.

In May 1903 King Edward VII paid a three-day visit to Paris. This was a triumphant success. The boos and 'Vivent les Boers!' of the first day were turned to cheers. 'One Anglophobe gloomily remarked: "I do not know what has happened to the population of Paris. The first day they behaved well; the second day they simply showed a little interest; but the third day it was really heart-breaking—they acclaimed the King!".' Edward VII did not make the Entente. World events drove the two countries together, and the politicians concerned, principally Delcassé and Lansdowne, drew the necessary conclusions. But in three days the King had altered the whole climate of Anglo-French relations. He did it by his qualities as a man: his unforced dignity, his geniality and his flair for handling people, all, on this occasion, warmed by his genuine and long-standing love of Paris. President Loubet paid a return visit to London in July. Delcassé took the opportunity to open negotiations in a talk with Lansdowne, whom he found receptive. So was Balfour, who reported to the King that the Cabinet was unanimous in wanting to proceed with the negotiations on the basis outlined by Delcassé. Lansdowne had a series of talks with Cambon at the end of July and the beginning of August.

Detailed negotiations began in October under a series of war clouds—in Macedonia, Tibet and China. That in China was the most menacing. On 12 December Russia made new proposals about Manchuria that the Japanese foreign minister described as 'most unsatisfactory'. Tension mounted. Lansdowne appealed again to the U.S.A. to act as mediator, and this time to France too. Neither would act. He then wanted to put the maximum pressure on Japan to accept 'the best bargain they can get as to Korea'. But Balfour and the Cabinet would not support him, and he could do nothing. None of the politicians had any confidence in their Japanese ally; their attitudes were all based on the expectation of a Russian victory. Only the War Office partially dissented: it was pro-Japanese, because it feared Britain might be faced with a war against Russia and France with Japan already crushed; but it believed that the 'British and Japanese fleets would have no difficulty in mastering their opponents'. War broke out on 8 February with the Japanese attack on the Russian ships in Port Arthur. This gave an impetus to the negotiations in London.

The Anglo-French Agreement was signed on 8 April 1904. It cleared up all the minor sources of friction between the two Powers, in Africa, south-east Asia, the Pacific and the Newfoundland fisheries; it gave France the Iles de Los off French Guinea and parts of the Gambia and northern Nigeria; and it settled the related problems of Egypt and Morocco. France recognised the

British occupation of Egypt and promised support for Cromer's financial reforms; Britain promised support for the measures France might have to undertake to preserve order in Morocco. But secret clauses providing that, when the Sultan's authority collapsed, northern Morocco with the Mediterranean coast should go to Spain, indicated that the two Powers expected that time would eliminate the Sultan and that France would take his place.

Reactions to the agreement varied. The French colonialists regarded it almost exclusively as an agreement to give France a free hand in Morocco. Delcassé saw it not only in this light and as a settlement of old disputes, but also as a possible agent in bringing about a new alignment in international affairs. But he was cautious as well as hopeful: he encouraged the Russians to complete the Orenburg-Tashkent railway as a means of keeping the pressure on Britain in central Asia; and he maintained the defences and arms factories in Algeria and Tunisia in case they were cut off from France by sea. Chamberlain and most Foreign Office officials valued the agreement as a check on Germany; Bülow agreed with them and planned his actions accordingly (see below, p. 80). Balfour, on the other hand, preoccupied with India, regarded it primarily as a means of getting better relations with Russia through France. Lansdowne was of the same opinion, though less alarmed for India than Balfour. From this point of view the first-fruits were not long in coming, for by May Russia had agreed to support the abolition of the *Caisse de la Dette* in Egypt in return for a British promise of non-intervention in Tibet, so long as no other Power intervened.

The value of Russia as an ally was however made doubtful by the destruction of the Russian Navy. The Russian Far Eastern fleet was crippled by the initial Japanese attack on Port Arthur in February 1904. The Baltic fleet sailed to do duty in its place. En route on the night of 21 October it mistook some trawlers of the Hull fishing fleet for Japanese warships and opened fire. It sank one ship and damaged several others. It then proceeded on its way without picking up survivors or wirelessing news of the engagement. Indignation in Britain was very great. The Cabinet was highly excited. But Lansdowne remained cool, and his ambassador in St. Petersburg worked hard for peace; above all Russia could not afford to add Britain to Japan at this juncture. Russia gave satisfaction and the crisis passed. The Baltic fleet sailed on to its doom in the straits of Tsushima on 25 May 1905. At a blow the German Navy replaced the Russian as the third largest in the world: the two-Power Standard that had till this moment applied to France and Russia now applied to France and Germany.

4 Strategy and naval policy   'You know,' Arthur Balfour said to his niece and biographer, Blanche Dugdale, 'Uncle Robert never paid any attention to these things [matters of co-operation between the services in defence of the country]—his mind didn't work on those questions, they didn't bite on it.' Salisbury (Uncle Robert) indeed paid no attention to these things. Nor did Grey, Peel, Disraeli or Gladstone. This was partly due to the cast of their minds, but still more to the situation of the country. Britain was protected by the Channel and the navy, and did not expect to use troops except in India and in occasional colonial expeditions. There was no need for a grand strategy or for regular co-ordination of the policies of the Admiralty and the War Office. Nothing more clearly shows the changed situation of Britain than the setting up of the Committee of Imperial Defence in 1902.

This replaced the old and ineffective defence committee of the Cabinet, and its constitution and its purpose were quite different. It consisted not of certain members of the Cabinet but of those who were summoned by the Prime Minister to advise him on problems of imperial defence—normally the parliamentary and service chiefs of the navy and the army and their expert advisers, together with anyone else specially summoned and including Dominion representatives. The Prime Minister was in the chair. It had from the start a permanent secretariat to assist it: to prepare agenda, to take minutes of the meetings and to provide continuity of organisation and policy between the meetings of the committee. Its purpose is well defined in the words of a memorandum submitted to Balfour in November 1902, signed jointly by the First Lord of the Admiralty and the Secretary of

State for War: to consider with authority the 'most difficult and important problems of all, viz.: those which were neither purely naval, nor purely military, nor purely naval and military combined, but which may be described as naval, military and political'. The committee owed its origin to the muddle occasioned and revealed by the South African War, which impressed itself forcibly on the minds of able officers, from the navy and army alike. But it is doubtful whether it would have taken shape so quickly but for Balfour. He was shocked by discovering how ineffective the Cabinet was at co-ordinating the war effort. His mind, unlike his uncle's, did work 'on those questions', and he had the necessary constructive imagination and administrative drive to set up a working organisation. As Prime Minister he was in the strongest position not only to set it up, but to get it working and to give it status and direction from the very beginning. 'We began', in his own words, 'on the particular subject—the defence of these Islands.' But it is significant of the pace of the work and of Britain's changed situation that by the autumn of 1905 it was considering the strategic implications of a possible Anglo-French war with Germany.

Significant too of the changed situation are the naval reforms known as the Cawdor-Fisher reforms, though they might more properly be called the Selborne-Cawdor-Fisher reforms, as they were initiated in 1904-5 during the terms of office as First Lord of the Admiralty of the Earl of Selborne and Earl Cawdor.

There were two crucial features of the reforms that affected strategy and foreign policy. The first was the policy of fleet concentration. Fisher ruthlessly scrapped obsolete ships, which he called 'floating deathtraps' and which were eking out their last days in remote waters. He withdrew ships from far-flung bases, where they were in his opinion of no use, and from cruising in various parts of the world, 'showing the flag', an occupation, in his view, overrated. He concentrated three-quarters of the fleet in European waters, in three commands: a Mediterranean Command based on Malta, an Atlantic Command based on Gibraltar and a Channel Command based on home ports. Setting up the Atlantic Command involved taking half the existing Mediterranean Fleet out of the Mediterranean and trusting the French Navy to undertake the duties it had previously fulfilled. The reasons for this policy were technical, and they were soundly based on the principles of strategy (and incidentally of economics). But their implications for foreign policy are obvious. A navy concentrated in the Channel, in the Eastern Atlantic and the Mediterranean could be intended to protect these islands only against the French or the German Navy—and after the achievement of the Entente Cordiale it was not the French.

Secondly there was the decision to build new types of battleship and battle cruiser, each much faster and more heavily gunned than any ship afloat. The keel of the prototype battleship, H.M.S. *Dreadnought*, was laid down in October 1905 and she was completed in December 1906; the prototype cruiser, H.M.S. *Invincible*, and two sister ships were included in the programme for 1905–6. The decision to build the *Dreadnought* was a controversial one; it gave rise to much criticism at the time and has been a matter for argument ever since. The case against it was stated with force by Lloyd George in 1908: 'We said, let there be dreadnoughts. What for? We did not require them. Nobody was building them, and if anyone had started building them, we, with our greater shipbuilding resources, could have built them faster than any other country in the world.' It is unquestionably true that one dreadnought devalued all old battleships. Germany saw this at once and drew the conclusion that she now had a chance to overtake Britain and that she must take it. This meant that there must be a naval arms race between the two Powers, which Britain had started by a deliberate policy decision. This is a heavy charge to face in view of the threat to the country's safety posed by a superior German fleet. But the risk of not building the *Dreadnought* was at least as great. Lloyd George was correct in saying that in 1905 nobody was building such a ship, but not in the implication that nobody had thought of building one. On the contrary, suggestions for a larger battleship were already in the air in a number of foreign countries, including Austria-Hungary, Italy, Japan and the U.S.A. This almost certainly meant that one would be built somewhere; and it was not impossible that, given good security arrangements, it might be built in secret, and that a foreign Power might in this way get a head start. Could any British government have taken so great a risk? Beyond this there were two further arguments that supported the case for building: no ship of dreadnought dimensions could get through the Kiel Canal, and to take her battleships to and from the Baltic to the North Sea Germany would have to reconstruct it completely; since the British government had the initiative it could decide the pace of naval construction. These two arguments interlock. To reconstruct the Kiel Canal would take time; and the reconstruction would give time for the dreadnoughts to be built. The German admiralty saw the point at once: the Navy Law of April 1906 authorised the widening of the canal. But the canal was not ready until six weeks before the outbreak of the war in August 1914. The Cawdor-Fisher programme laid down four dreadnoughts in 1906, four in 1907 and so on until further notice. 'Therefore,' reckons Ensor, 'Great Britain would have had a fleet of ten, and perhaps fourteen, dreadnoughts or *Invincibles* afloat before a single German ship of their class had been completed; and a start would have been established which nothing could overtake.' That this was not established was the responsibility of the Liberal government that came into power in December 1905 and cut the Cawdor-Fisher programme (see below, p. 92).

Chapter IV

The foreign policy of Sir Edward Grey

1 Personality and principles Sir Edward Grey, Bart. (1862–1933, created Viscount Grey of Fallodon 1916) was born in London, 'and I have always felt', he wrote, 'that my six brothers and sisters had the advantage of me in that they were all not only brought up but born at Fallodon'. He was a kinsman of Earl Grey of the Reform Bill and was a countryman to the core. One day he remarked to G. M. Trevelyan, also a member of an old Northumberland family and later Grey's biographer, 'Oh yes, I wanted to talk to you about old Lord Grey. People used to praise him and Lord Althorp because they were such fine fellows and passed such a good Bill. Then they used to say it was such a pity that Grey always wanted to be away in Northumberland, and Althorp in Northamptonshire. But that was just the reason why they did so well whenever they were in London.' (*Grey of Fallodon*, p. v.) When Parliament was in session Grey could not easily get away to Fallodon, but he escaped at the week-ends to his cottage by the Itchen or went walking in the New Forest with sandwiches in his pocket.

He was an expert fisherman and ornithologist, and a naturalist with a sharp eye. 'There are a few days in the first part of May', he writes in his *Twenty-Five Years*, 'when the beech trees in young leaf give an aspect of light and tender beauty to English country which is well known but indescribable. The days are very few; the colour of the leaves soon darkens, their texture becomes stiffer; beautiful they are, still, but "the glory and the dream" are gone.'

Grey goes on to relate how in the year 1906 he was prevented from going down to his accustomed wood on what he called 'Beech Sunday' by the necessity of staying in London to wait for the reply to a British ultimatum to Sultan Abdul Hamid. This was almost more than Grey could bear, and he expressed his feelings to one of his officials at the Foreign Office. 'He listened civilly, but, as was told me years afterwards, expressed outside my room astonishment that was scornful.'

Everyone who met Grey or had to deal with him agreed with the German ambassador, Metternich, that he was 'a frank, straightforward man, that one knows where one is with him'. But he was also markedly reserved in his conduct of foreign policy, or, in Zara Steiner's phrase, 'in marked contrast to his immediate predecessors . . . far from open in his dealings with other ministers'. In his first years he consulted no one but the Prime Minister, Campbell-Bannerman, and Ripon, the doyen of the Liberal party; and sent important despatches to no one but the King and these two ministers. (For examples, see G. E. Monger, *The End of Isolation*, pp. 307–8.) This sprang in part from Grey's independent, self-reliant character, in part from the fact that the Cabinet as a whole was immersed in home affairs, and with the exception of Morley at the India Office, who luckily saw eye to eye with Grey from the Indian angle and more than once deputised for him at the Foreign Office when he was on holiday, the leading Radical members of the Cabinet were all in home departments: Loreburn, Bryce, John Burns, Harcourt, Lloyd George. Further it is to be remembered that since Salisbury's resignation the Foreign Office had become a highly professional department with a jealous regard for its independence and a proper professional contempt for what it regarded as the loose and woolly vapourings of politicians and other outsiders.

Unlike Salisbury and to a greater extent than Lansdowne Grey consulted his officials; some of his critics thought he deferred to them too much. 'By disposition and temper', writes Mrs Steiner, 'Grey was the kind of chief who solicited and welcomed advice and even encouraged adverse criticism. "Grey was always tolerant of opposition", Algernon Law said of his former chief. "He liked to hear and weigh arguments against a line of conduct which he was inclined to favour." ' But he was by no means in the hands of his officials: his relations with his two successive Permanent Under-Secretaries, Hardinge and Nicolson, show this conclusively.

The fundamentals of British foreign policy remained what they had been throughout the nineteenth century, and Grey subscribed to them; the difference lay in the setting. The international scene was changed by the, perhaps temporary, eclipse of Russia, the emergence of Germany on the world stage and the Entente Cordiale with France. Grey formulated his policy accordingly. He was absolutely determined to stand by France. He was 'impatient to see Russia re-established as a factor in European politics'. He looked forward to an agreement with Russia that would complement and extend the Entente with France. He wanted to pursue friendly relations with Germany provided Germany acquiesced in Britain's friendly relations with France and Russia.

The domestic scene was changed by the much increased self-consciousness and vociferousness of public opinion; by the strength within the Liberal party of the neutralists; and by the emergence of the Labour party and of a small, but not negligible, pacifist group. Grey was at all times highly conscious of this. He believed in 1906, and he never deviated from this belief, that it was impossible to turn the Entente into an alliance as the French wished. As he told the French ambassador, Paul Cambon, 'Should such a defensive alliance be formed, it was too serious a matter to be kept secret from Parliament. The Government could conclude it without the assent of Parliament, but it would have to be published afterwards. No British Government could commit the country to such a serious thing and keep the engagement secret.' And he did not believe that the country would have swallowed such an alliance in 1906, or even in 1914. Speaking in the House of Lords on the occasion of Asquith's death in 1928 he recalled the last days of July 1914 and put his conviction into these words: 'But if the Prime Minister, as Asquith then was, had precipitated a decision to bring Great Britain into the war on the side of

France, I believe the consequences would have been that at the moment of crisis we should have had a divided Government, a divided Parliament, a divided country.' All his policy is contained in this: to cultivate friendly relations with all the Powers, but to ensure that, if war came, Britain should face it as a united country.

2 The testing of the Entente   The news of the conclusion of the Entente in April 1904 was vexatious to Germany. The Kaiser reacted by trying to bring off an alliance with Russia. When this failed he was forced by Bülow to try and break up the Entente by intervention in Morocco. Delcassé had provided the German government with a cast-iron excuse for this by leaving Germany out of the Moroccan arrangements, although by the terms of the Treaty of Madrid (1880) she had as much right to be consulted as Spain, Italy and Britain. The German intervention took the melodramatic form of the Kaiser landing at Tangier and making a speech in which he emphasised the independence of the Sultan of Morocco and his intention of dealing with him direct over German interests. The object of this gesture was, in Bülow's words, 'to confront France with the possibility of war, cause Delcassé's fall, break the continuity of aggressive French policy, knock the continental dagger out of the hands of Edward VII and the war group in England and, simultaneously, ensure peace, preserve German honour and improve German prestige'. This rodomontade justifies A. J. P. Taylor's comment (p. 428): 'The Germans had no clear idea what they meant to do when they butted into Morocco. They wished to show that Germany could not be ignored in any question in the world. More vaguely, they hoped to weaken the Anglo-French entente or perhaps to shake the Franco-Russian alliance. But essentially they speculated on some undefined success.'

At the end of the year the Conservatives resigned and Campbell-Bannerman formed a Liberal government with Asquith as Chancellor of the Exchequer, Grey as Foreign Secretary and Haldane as Secretary of State for War—three close friends, labelled 'Liberal imperialists', in leading posts. They were however balanced by Loreburn, the Lord Chancellor, Lloyd

George at the Board of Trade and, most importantly, by Campbell-Bannerman himself as Prime Minister, all of whom were anti-imperialist and in varying degrees 'Little Englanders'. The Prime Minister obtained a dissolution of Parliament, and the general election, then spread over several weeks, took place during January 1906.

Grey was plunged at once into the Moroccan crisis. On 3 January he saw Metternich, the German ambassador in London. He warned him that the Entente was popular in England and that there was a general feeling that England could not leave France in the lurch; this contention has been disputed by Earl Loreburn in *How the War Came* (Methuen, 1919), where he argues that 'the House of Commons elected in January 1906 [showed] a strong resentment at the Imperialist War in South Africa' and infers that 'public opinion would [by no means] have rallied to the material support of France'. 'Later in the conversation', reported Metternich, 'Sir Edward Grey said he had found among his predecessor's memoranda a conversation with me in the previous summer, in which Lord Lansdowne indicated that, if there was war between Germany and France on account of Morocco, public feeling would force the government to fight for France. He, Grey, believed that the British people would not stand France being involved in war with Germany on account of the Anglo-French agreement, and that, if it happened, any British Government, whether Conservative or Liberal, would be forced to help France.' Grey confirmed Metternich's account of this conversation to Lascelles in Berlin and to the Prime Minister.

A week later, on 10 January, Grey saw Paul Cambon. He assured him of British diplomatic support. But when Cambon asked him whether, in the event of attack by Germany, France could rely on armed support, Grey said he could not answer; owing to the election he could not even consult the Prime Minister or the Cabinet. But he gave it as his 'personal opinion that if France were to be attacked by Germany, public opinion would be strongly moved in favour of France'. Cambon went on to say that he did not think there would be war, but that it would make it certain that there would not be, if William II knew that

Britain would fight. Grey answered that William probably did know this, (for Grey had conveyed a warning to him through Metternich only a week before) but it was one thing to warn Germany and quite another to give a promise to France. This was consistently Grey's line: he would do his utmost to back the Entente, which he strongly approved and believed to be a factor for peace in Europe, but he would not give a promise he was sure that neither the Cabinet, nor Parliament, nor the country would, at the critical moment, honour.

Later in the conversation Cambon suggested that it was advisable that unofficial military and naval conversations between the two staffs should take place. 'Some communications had, he believed, already passed, and might, he thought, be continued. They did not pledge either Government.' 'I did not dissent from this view', reported Grey to the British ambassador in Paris on the same evening.

On 31 January Grey, who in the meantime had been re-elected to Parliament, saw Cambon again. He repeated what he had said on 10 January, but amplified it. He told Cambon of his talk with Metternich on 3 January and added that he believed that Metternich's despatch had had the desired effect. He said that the military talks were in progress. Cambon was not satisfied with this, as he feared there might be another German threat of war, and this might mean 'war might arrive so suddenly that the need for action would be a question not of days, but of minutes', and there was accordingly a need for an assurance of military support from Britain. Grey thereupon explained that such an assurance would amount to a defensive alliance, and would have to be submitted to Parliament. He then again reiterated his personal opinion that if 'it appeared that the war was forced on France by Germany to break up the Anglo-French "Entente", public opinion would undoubtedly be very strong on the side of France'.

In the event it did not come to war. German diplomacy had had a certain success. It frightened the French Cabinet into abandoning Delcassé, who was forced to resign. Through President Roosevelt it had forced France to accept an international conference to consider the Moroccan Question as a whole. The conference opened at Algeciras in January 1906. It was a sad disappointment to Germany. American pressure had played its part in bringing the conference into existence, but it was not sustained on behalf of the demands Germany put forward. Nor were these backed by Germany's supposed ally in the Triple Alliance, Italy. During January and February there was prolonged argument over the control of the Moroccan police. At the beginning of March it became clear that only Austria-Hungary and Morocco gave Germany any support. Bülow realised that Germany was isolated and gave way. The protocol of the conference signed on 7 April 1906 retained the formal rule of the Sultan, but gave the practical control of the Moroccan Bank to France, and of the police to France and Spain jointly.

The Sultan remained, Delcassé was gone. This was the extent of the German achievement. The French continued to absorb Morocco. The Entente Cordiale emerged the stronger from this baptism of fire. German honour was shown in a doubtful light; German prestige suffered. Grey himself thought that, apart from preserving peace, there were two results of the conference of the greatest importance: first, it had shown President Roosevelt to be a staunch supporter of the Entente and thereby confirmed Grey's faith in Anglo-American friendship, 'based on a fundamental oneness of outlook which he believed to exist'; secondly, Britain's firmness in sticking to the Entente had made a clear impression on Russia. This he hoped could be made the foundation of an agreement with Russia to supplement that with France.

Of equal importance for the future of British foreign policy was Grey's authorisation of the naval and military staff conversations. When Grey took over the Foreign Office from Lansdowne he found that naval and military conversations between France and Britain were in progress. The French naval attaché had been in official touch with the First Sea Lord, and Grey assumed that Fisher had 'all naval plans prepared', though in fact he was wrong in this assumption (see A. J. Marder, *From the Dreadnought to Scapa Flow*, vol 1, p. 117). The military conversations were on a yet more unofficial footing, and after consulting Haldane Grey authorised them to proceed on an official level. The Prime

Minister was informed only on his return to London from Scotland at the end of January. He was, according to Sir George Clarke, the Secretary of the Committee of Imperial Defence, 'not at all inclined to be alarmed at what I told him we had done', and did not see fit to inform the Cabinet. For this decision and for approving the conversations the Prime Minister must bear the ultimate responsibility, but it is natural and proper that Grey as Foreign Secretary has borne his full share of it. He has been much criticised on two counts. First, he did not get Cabinet approval for the conversations. Grey, who later came to believe that he ought to have sought and obtained this approval, himself gave as his excuse for not doing this that it was impossible at the time owing to the general election. This is not wholly convincing, for Grey saw Campbell-Bannerman at Windsor on his return from Scotland and a Cabinet was held on 31 January. Cambon believed that the King, the Prime Minister and Grey had agreed to keep silent and not inform the Cabinet. This is not impossible, though there is no evidence for the belief. Loreburn later suggested that there was a cabal of Grey, Haldane and Asquith to make a decision and withhold it from the Cabinet. As Ensor says, the fact that Grey consulted the Prime Minister disposes of this suggestion. He thinks a more likely explanation is the need for secrecy and the risk of a leak from a relatively large Cabinet. Possibly Grey's training at the Foreign Office under Rosebery and his respect for its traditions may have contributed to his decision.

The second reason for criticising Grey is for having authorised the military conversations at all. The argument is that holding military conversations implies turning an entente into an alliance. It cannot be denied that holding conversations involves naming a hypothetical enemy; conversations about the general situation without planning operations against a particular Power would be mere beating the air. Of course the assumed enemy was Germany, and, as is well known, Haldane's war plans involved putting an expeditionary force on the left flank of the French army on the outbreak of war. On the other hand it was doubtful up to the last minute whether Britain would enter the war in 1914. The Germans expected her to remain neutral and the Cabinet was divided. It was the invasion of Belgium that ensured British action. Had there been no military or naval conversations Britain would still have entered the war; the only difference would have been that she would have entered it with no previously concerted plans. Looking at the conversations in the immediate context of 1906 the same point applies. There was an undoubted risk of war between Germany and France in 1906. Grey was clear that Britain must give France full diplomatic support to honour the Anglo-French agreement and to minimise the risk of war. Despite this war might come. France would in that event demand armed support from Britain. Most likely Britain would not have given it; in that event the conversations would have come to an end. Perhaps Britain would have given it; in that case the previous conversations would have made joint action both easier and quicker.

Grey never wavered in his belief that Britain must stand by France, but, as we have seen, he came to believe that he had been wrong in not bringing the matter of the military conversations before the Cabinet. The conversations came into the open in 1912 and were then fully debated by the Cabinet. It gave its sanction to them and decided that the conditions governing them should be put in writing. It then drafted a letter that Grey sent to Cambon. This stated that consultation did not constitute an engagement committing either government, but that 'if either Government had grave reason to expect an unprovoked attack by a third Power, it might become essential to know whether it could, in that event, depend upon the armed assistance of the other. I agree that, if either Government had grave reason to expect an unprovoked attack by a third Power, or something that threatened the general peace, it should immediately discuss with the other whether both Governments should act together to prevent aggression and to preserve peace, and, if so, what measures they would be prepared to take in common. If these measures involved action, the plans of the general staffs would at once be taken into consideration, and the Governments would then decide what effect should be given to them.' Cambon accepted this statement of the position next day.

3 Diplomacy for peace and preparation for war For a new Foreign Secretary to be plunged into crisis immediately on taking office can be no trivial experience, and it would be natural for him to lean heavily on his professional advisers and to follow his predecessor's policy unless he was overwhelmingly convinced that it was contrary to his country's interests. In the circumstances Grey might, almost inadvertently, have prejudiced his future freedom of action as Foreign Secretary. This was, however, not so, for Grey did not come unprepared to his office. As Parliamentary Under-Secretary for Foreign Affairs under Rosebery he had formed 'the general impression . . . that we were expected to give way whenever British interests conflicted with German interests, and that we got no diplomatic support from Germany anywhere and continual friction'. Further he remembered that 'the position was anything but comfortable, and that we appeared destined to be for ever on bad terms with France and Russia, with Germany as a "tertius gaudens" '.

Grey wholeheartedly welcomed the Entente with France and was determined that, as far as lay in his power, relations between the two countries should never relapse into their former uneasy, and often hostile, state, but should be frank, cordial and co-operative. His language and his conduct were clear and consistent: he assured Cambon of diplomatic support and he was as good as his word. He was also convinced that diplomatic support was of value only to the extent that it was backed by effective military power. He was therefore a consistent supporter of Fisher's naval reforms, concentrating the fleet in home waters and maintaining British naval superiority over Germany (see p. 74f), and of Haldane's army reforms, which appealed to Grey the Radical as much as to Grey the Foreign Secretary. For Haldane achieved the remarkable feat of saving money on the army estimates, and so releasing it for expenditure on social reforms, while at the same time providing the country with a far more efficient and flexible army than ever before. He created a general staff for military planning and for the direction of war, should war occur; he planned and built up a force of six infantry divisions and one cavalry division, complete with artillery, transport and medical units, capable of rapid mobilisation and despatch to an overseas theatre of war; he merged the old militia and volunteers into a Territorial Force to form a reserve that could rapidly go into action in support of the expeditionary force of the regular army; and he converted the old rifle corps in schools into the Officers Training Corps, which, in Ensor's words, 'helped materially towards solving the hard problem of officering the "new armies" during the European war'.

When France was subjected to another bout of pressure by Germany over Morocco in 1911 Grey's diplomacy was much strengthened by knowledge of these reforms and by the Russian backing that followed from the Franco-Russian Alliance and from the Anglo-Russian Entente (see below, p. 90). In March 1911 France moved troops towards Fez in support of the Sultan of Morocco against rebels. Germany seems to have decided that this was a situation out of which she could make capital and demonstrate her status as a Great Power. Towards the end of April the German Foreign Secretary, Kiderlen-Wächter, warned France that if French troops stayed too long Germany would consider herself to have entire freedom of action (whatever that might mean). The German government then lapsed into ominous silence. Two months later, during which French troops had occupied Fez, it sent a German warship, the *Panther*, to Agadir on the Atlantic coast of Morocco, where it anchored on 1 July.

The British government was nonplussed. It could not make out what Germany was up to. It inclined to the view that she wanted to get such excessive compensation for acquiescing in French control of Morocco, under threat of war, that she would humiliate France and disrupt the Entente. British public opinion was much agitated at the idea of Germany seizing a base on the Atlantic coast of Morocco, and the Permanent Under-Secretary at the Foreign Office, Nicolson, was also impressed by the danger. But the Admiralty scouted the idea, for Agadir was 1,500 miles from German home waters and there were no good anchorages on the coast, though it insisted at the same time that Germany should on no account be allowed to acquire a base on the Mediterranean coast. Germany followed up her action by claiming the whole of the French Congo as compensation—possibly a confirmation of the British view. Grey supported France, but made it clear that the British government expected France to give some compensation to Germany, preferably outside Morocco. He was also careful to state that Britain would fight only for British interests (in this case to keep Germany away from Tangier and the Mediterranean coast opposite Gibraltar). At the same time he told Metternich that he thought 'British commercial interests were... considerably larger than German in Morocco and reasons given for German action would apply at least as strongly to us'. A few days later he repeated this statement in the House of Commons. 'It was an indirect invitation to Germany to make her intentions clear.' Instead Germany maintained a loud silence.

On 21 July Lloyd George came to see Grey and suggested he should insert a warning to Germany in the speech he was to give at a Mansion House banquet that evening. Grey approved, as did Asquith; no other member of the Cabinet was consulted. The warning Lloyd George gave was unambiguous: 'I believe it is essential in the highest interests, not only of this country, but of the world, that Britain should at all hazards maintain her place and prestige among the Great Powers of the world. ... If a situation were to be forced upon us in which peace could only be preserved by the surrender of the great and beneficent position Britain has won by centuries of heroism and achievement, by allowing herself to be treated, where her interests were vitally affected, as if she were of no account in the Cabinet of nations, then I say emphatically that peace at that price would be a humiliation intolerable for a great country like ours to endure. National honour is no party question.'

The speech made the more impression coming from a known neutralist and friend of Germany. It was received with approval in England, in many quarters with enthusiasm; with resentment in Germany. Its ultimate effect on the German government is doubtful. Grey was so alarmed by Metternich's expression of the German government's anger that he at once sent for Lloyd George and Churchill and told them: 'I have just received a communication from the German Ambassador so stiff that the Fleet might be

attacked at any moment. I have sent for McKenna to warn him.'
This from a man of stoical endurance and a notably cool head.
However, the German fleet did not attack and the crisis persisted.
It was not until the autumn that detailed negotiations led to the
Franco-German Agreement signed on 4 November 1911. By this
Germany recognised a French protectorate over Morocco; France
ceded to Germany a considerable part of the Congo. G. M.
Trevelyan writes of the Mansion House Speech, 'It caused wild
indignation in Germany that almost led to war; but in fact it
proved the road to peace.' This seems to be going beyond the
evidence. The grim German reaction, the sustained crisis, the
long-drawn-out negotiations and the stiff compensation demanded
suggest a sustained tough attitude rather than one of frightened
anger. It is possible that the effect of the speech was less deterrent
than provocative.

The agreement itself was a bad bargain for Germany. Its
consequences were worse. In France it brought about the fall of
the pro-German politician Caillaux and his replacement as Prime
Minister by Poincaré, a Lorrainer and one of the ablest and
toughest opponents of Germany. German frustration led to
successful pressure by Tirpitz for a supplementary naval law,
laying down three extra dreadnoughts, an increase designed, as
William II said in a speech at Hamburg, 'so that we can be sure
that no one will dispute our rightful place in the sun'. This new
law coming on top of the arrogant German attitude over Agadir
brought over to Grey's side the two ablest and most politically
powerful radicals, Lloyd George and Churchill, who succeeded
McKenna as First Lord of the Admiralty in October 1911. Finally
France's success in Morocco encouraged Italy to attack Turkey in
September 1911 in order to gain control of Tripoli. This was a
further blow to Germany, who since 1894 had steadily increased
her influence at Constantinople and was now unquestionably the
dominant Power.

From his first days in office Grey had been anxious to 'get and
keep on good terms' with Russia, and as early as February 1906 he
had written, 'I am impatient to see Russia re-established as a
factor in European politics.' His motives were general and

particular: he regarded an agreement with a great Power as a work of liberalism and peace, and, so long as relations with Russia were bad, he experienced a certain anxiety at a powerful Germany on the flank of British communications to India and the Far East. Grey accordingly responded with prompt cordiality to Russian overtures. The moment was propitious. Russia's defeat in the war with Japan had caused her to draw in her horns in the Far East and so remove one of the most vigorous of the causes of friction with Britain; and it had for the time being somewhat checked the Russian enthusiasm for a forward policy in Asia. Furthermore the new Russian foreign minister Izvolsky was strongly pro-British.

The chief stumbling-block to the negotiations was Persia. Conditions in Persia, as in Morocco, were unstable. Britain and Russia each had a strategic interest in the country, each had reason to fear the other and each had a case for intervention in Persian affairs. The Russian Government of Central Asia was as keen as the Government of India on absorbing the whole of Persia. But larger considerations prevailed. The Anglo-Russian Agreement of 31 August 1907 achieved a compromise. It divided Persia into three zones: in the north a Russian sphere of influence, in the south-east, adjoining Afghanistan and India, a British sphere of influence, and, in between, a neutral sphere. The zones were drawn on purely strategic grounds; it later turned out that Persian oil was more easily accessible to Britain. In addition both Powers recognised the independence and territorial integrity of Tibet under Chinese suzerainty, thus treating Tibet as a buffer state between them; and Russia agreed to conduct its relations with Afghanistan through Great Britain, thus recognising Afghanistan's status as a dependent of British India.

This agreement did not end all friction between the Powers, and Grey wrote much later that Persia caused him more trouble than any other problem during his years at the Foreign Office. Nor did it mean that Britain gave Russia automatic support in all international questions that arose: for example consideration for the new and supposedly constitutional 'Young Turk' government at Constantinople prevented Grey supporting Russia in the Bosnian crisis of 1908 when Izvolsky demanded the opening of the

Straits to Russian warships. But the agreement altered the pattern and atmosphere of the international scene. It brought about a détente in Anglo-Russian relations. It confirmed the Russian government's rejection of the Kaiser's offer of an alliance in 1905 and buttressed the Franco-Russian Alliance; the two agreements drew the three governments gradually together into the *Triple Entente*. It also had the probably unintentional effect of re-focusing Russia's attention on the Balkans in pursuit of her long-term goal, a warm-water port. The Treaty of Portsmouth had checked Russian expansion in the Yellow Sea; the Anglo-Russian Agreement had barred Russia from the Persian Gulf and the Indian Ocean; there remained the Straits, Constantinople and the Mediterranean. This situation foreshadowed renewed conflict with Austria-Hungary, and, behind her, Germany.

4 Negotiations with Germany   But being on good terms with France and Russia did not entail for Grey being on bad terms with Germany. On the contrary he believed that the settlement of points of conflict between Britain on the one hand and France and Russia on the other should make it easier, given goodwill and patience, to settle points of conflict between Britain and Germany and bring about an improvement in their relations. He worked steadily to this end and had a certain limited success. By 1914 prolonged negotiations had brought about agreements on the Baghdad railway and the Portuguese colonies in Africa, by which each country undertook to respect and further the other's interests. As neither agreement had been ratified by Germany when the war broke out, it is impossible to be sure how far the German government took them seriously and intended to honour them, or looked on them primarily as tactical moves in the international game. Grey regarded them as means of satisfying Germany's legitimate interests without sacrificing anything essential to Britain; the most telling criticism of Grey's policy is that he was not so much satisfying Germany's interests as encouraging her appetite.

Either way these are minor matters. What stood in the way of friendlier relations between the two Powers was naval rivalry and

Germany's insistence on British neutrality in the event of a continental war. Grey was as conscious of sea power as any British Foreign Secretary. It was an axiom of his policy that 'what really determines foreign policy in this country is the question of sea power'.

The first German naval programmes of 1898 and 1900 had not aroused much interest in Britain, and what there was had been obscured by the excitements and passions of the South African War. On the conclusion of the war the British government was conscious that the country was dangerously isolated, and, as we have seen, cast about for ways of emerging from this isolation. By 1911 the situation was quite different. The Entente Cordiale was in existence and, with Grey as its champion, had emerged strengthened from the Moroccan crises. Relations with the U.S.A. had much improved since Grey took office and Bryce had gone to Washington as ambassador. There was not the slightest risk of a naval war between the two countries, and in 1911 their governments signed a mutual arbitration treaty, unhappily not ratified by the U.S. Senate. Britain was the ally of Japan. Despite some friction between Japan and the British Dominions caused by the prospect of massive Japanese immigration the British government renewed the alliance with Japan for a further ten years in July 1911. British naval policy in the Far East was based on the alliance: Britain to a great extent looked to Japan to police Far Eastern waters.

Britannia still ruled the waves. But, as we have seen, she had already provoked a challenge to her supremacy by the construction of the *Dreadnought* in 1906. Unfortunately the Liberal government under Campbell-Bannerman in a praiseworthy but, as can now be seen, misguided desire to give a lead to international disarmament in preparation for the Second Hague Conference on Disarmament had given Germany material assistance in her challenge by cutting a dreadnought, among other things, from the naval construction programme of 1906. It cut another next year. In reply Germany shortened the life of her existing battleships and planned to replace each obsolete ship with one of the dreadnought type. The effect of this was that Germany would have nine dreadnoughts in the spring of 1911 to the British twelve. But this was not the worst of it from the British angle. There was great anxiety that the Germans could accelerate their building programme and, unless the British government did the same, pass the British total. It was calculated that by accelerating the 1909–10 programme the Germans could have not nine, but eleven, dreadnoughts by the autumn of 1911.

The Cabinet was divided. The Radicals did not believe that Germany was a menace and were most anxious to reduce the naval estimates, which they regarded as extravagant, so as to have more to spend on the great programme of social reforms they cared for so passionately, and to which the Cabinet and the party were committed. The Liberal imperialists, especially Grey and McKenna, who became First Lord of the Admiralty at the same time as Asquith succeeded Campbell-Bannerman as Prime Minister in April 1908, were deeply concerned by the naval challenge from Germany and were clear that it was a matter of life and death for Britain to maintain her naval superiority.

Grey was as devoted to the reforms as Lloyd George, but he was sure that the money for them must not be found at the expense of the navy. A possible way out of this dilemma seemed to be to persuade the German government to limit or slow up its naval building programme, which Grey also believed would serve to lessen the tension between the two countries. So he devoted much time and energy to this object: first at the Second Peace Conference at the Hague in 1907, where his efforts came to nothing, as the Germans regarded them as typical British hypocrisy, and were determined to have nothing to do with the limitation of armaments; then, throughout 1908, in talks with the German ambassador and through Edward VII, who had a meeting with William II in Germany in August. William II refused to discuss the limitation of the German naval programme. 'There comes a time in the history of every state', to misquote Woodward, 'when it is practically impossible, whatever the logical possibilities, to make a sudden and violent change in the [policy] of the state. This revolutionary change was outside the range of possibilities in the German Empire.'

In the winter of 1908 the Admiralty had what it believed was reliable information indicating that Germany was anticipating its published naval building programme by collecting material for ships in advance of laying their keels and by placing contracts for ships before they had been authorised by vote in the Reichstag. It is not quite clear how far this evidence was reliable (see E. L. Woodward, Chapter X and A. J. Marder, *From the Dreadnought to Scapa Flow*, vol. 1, pp. 159–64, 177–9.) But it was widely believed and led to a violent press campaign. The Conservative party attacked the government with the utmost vigour and confidence. The Conservative M.P. George Wyndham coined the slogan, 'We want eight, and we won't wait.' What made matters worse from the point of view of the Cabinet and the Foreign Office was that Grey's repeated efforts to extract a denial of the allegations from the German government before the presentation of the naval estimates to the House of Commons in March 1909 met only with ominous silence. Eventually, within twenty-four hours of the debate in the House of Commons, Tirpitz authorised a statement affirming that Germany was not accelerating her programme, and that she would not have more than thirteen capital ships by the summer of 1912, but admitting that contracts had been placed for two ships in advance of the Reichstag vote, 'in order to secure better prices and to prevent the formation of a trust'.

The long delay and the apparently lame excuse for the allocation of contracts did nothing to lessen suspicion and distrust. In the House of Commons McKenna explained with great care what the Admiralty believed was at the moment the German building programme. But Balfour disputed his figures. Behind the dispute lay the suspicion that it was no longer safe to rely on the figures given by the German government to the Reichstag and subsequently published and, therefore, that it was no longer safe to plan British construction on the assumption that the German programme was known and would be kept to. In the circumstances the government had to allow for a possible German acceleration. It did not give in to the Conservative demand for eight dreadnoughts to be laid down in 1909, but it planned to lay down four, with the possibility of laying down four more than the House would already have authorised, should it become clear at any future time that Germany was in fact accelerating her programme. (Germany did not do so, but it has been plausibly argued that this was due to the publicity given to German construction in 1909.)

In the debate Grey made an important speech which sums up his attitude to the arms race and so contains a large part of his foreign policy. He began by stating that expenditure on armament now amounted to about half the revenue; if this continued it would submerge civilisation. But it was impossible for Britain to get out of this arms race, for simple withdrawal would lead to the loss of her self-respect. A nation without self-respect sinks into apathy and would be lucky if it were allowed to survive and not become the 'conscript appendage of some stronger Power'. Turning to the navies of Britain and Germany he echoed Balfour's dictum in these words: 'Our Navy is to us what their Army is to them.' There were only two things that could produce conflict between the two Powers: an attempt by Britain to isolate Germany, and an attempt by Germany to isolate Britain, 'so as to dominate and dictate the policy of the Continent'. There was at present undoubted tension between them. What could be done to lessen it? Diminish naval expenditure. *But* 'it must be on the basis of a superiority of the British Navy'.

The scare of 1909 died away, to a great extent because public opinion was diverted by Lloyd George's budget of 1909 and the government's consequent struggle with the House of Lords. But Grey pegged away at negotiation with Germany with a view to lessening tension and expenditure. During 1909 the negotiations were mainly political in character. Grey tried to get Germany to slow down her rate of building; Bülow tried to get Britain to give a promise of neutrality in the event of Germany being involved in a continental war. But the negotiations were at cross-purposes: Bülow, and the Kaiser, thought of them in terms of a bargain, in which Britain must pay a price (a promise of neutrality) for what she wanted (naval deceleration); Grey regarded as given facts that Britain had naval supremacy, that she was determined to keep it and that she could bear the financial strain of competitive building better than Germany. There was no question of a bargain in the German sense. What might be agreed was a mutual deceleration that would be of great benefit to both countries (though it might have meant increased German expenditure on the army, which would not have been welcome to Great Britain's continental friends).

In 1910 the negotiations were mainly technical: to try to establish the principle and practice of exchange of information by the two Powers on their naval building programmes. Here again there were different interpretations of what was meant by information and by simultaneity. Fundamentally neither Power trusted the other, and Germany was determined not to be limited in her sovereignty by any agreement or exchange of information. The negotiations were interrupted by the Agadir crisis. When the crisis was over the government made another attempt. In February 1912 Haldane went to Berlin on behalf of the Cabinet and saw William II, who had Tirpitz with him, and Bethmann-Hollweg, who had succeeded Bülow as Chancellor in July 1909 and wanted a political agreement with Britain. Unfortunately he was not strong enough to stand up to Tirpitz and the big navy group. The negotiations were a failure. Tirpitz would not consider any slowing down in the naval building programme; Bethmann and Haldane could not agree on a formula of neutrality; the fundamental incompatibility of the two points of view remained. On top of this, new misunderstandings arose over the cession of Zanzibar and Pemba, and over Haldane's powers—whether he had been given full powers by the Cabinet to conclude binding agreements (which he had not).

Even then the negotiations were not at an end. Throughout February and March the two governments tried to find a formula that would satisfy them both. Grey put forward a simple form of words that in his view exactly expressed the situation: 'England will make no unprovoked attack upon Germany and pursue no aggressive policy towards her. Aggression upon Germany is not the subject and forms no part of any Treaty understanding or combination to which England is now a party nor will she become a party to anything that has such an object.' Metternich suggested an addition that should run: 'England will therefore observe at least a benevolent neutrality should war be forced upon Germany' or 'England will therefore as a matter of course remain neutral if a war is forced upon Germany.' It was an impossibility. Germany was determined on extracting a pledge that Britain would remain neutral if war broke out between Germany and Russia or Germany and France, a war in which either Power might be technically the aggressor but which had been provoked by the aggressive policy of Germany, or perhaps of Germany's ally Austria-Hungary. Britain on the other hand was determined not to give any pledge that might be incompatible with her understandings with France and Russia and that might easily be repudiated by Parliament.

The failure to get an agreement with Germany was offset by arrangements with France and Russia. In the course of 1912 France decided to move her Atlantic fleet from Brest to Toulon to give her greater security against increases in the Austrian and Italian navies that were worrying her. She thus denuded her Atlantic seaboard and relied on torpedo craft and the British navy to protect it. There was no British promise of action in the event of enemy attack, and Winston Churchill, the First Lord of the Admiralty, told the House of Commons with his accustomed force that Britain retained full freedom of choice. But the fact remains that no French government could have taken this decision with any confidence, had it had serious doubts about British action in the event of attack by Germany. Naval conversations between the two Powers led to an agreement in 1913 on various technical arrangements, for example over signals, that would take effect *if* the two Powers were allies in war.

Finally in 1914 Grey, under pressure from France, sanctioned naval conversations with Russia. He was a trifle embarrassed over this but did not think that naval co-operation with Russia could amount to much. As he wrote later, 'I could see little if any strategic necessity or value in the suggestion. To my lay mind it seemed that, in a war against Germany, the Russian Fleet would not get out of the Baltic and the British Fleet would not get into it; but the difficulty of refusing was obvious.' It is impossible not to agree with Grey.

5 The coming of war In 1912 the focus of interest shifted suddenly to the Balkans once more. In the spring and early summer of 1912 Russian diplomacy brought about alliances between Serbia and Bulgaria, and Serbia and Greece. In October Montenegro declared war on Turkey, and Serbia, Bulgaria and Greece joined in. Their armies were rapidly successful; but it was one thing to gain victories on the battlefield, another to force the Turks to make peace quickly, something they were notorious for avoiding. But unless peace was made quickly there was a risk of the conflict turning into a European war: Russia might feel compelled to intervene to force the Sultan's hand, and this in turn might draw in Austria-Hungary to prevent the enlargement of Serbia and Montenegro. Grey regarded the situation as one peculiarly suited to joint diplomatic action by the Concert of Europe: the protagonists were minor states, the integrity of Turkey had throughout the nineteenth century been a concern of the Powers, and the vital interests of both Austria and Russia were affected. Fortunately Austria-Hungary's policy was confused and negative; Germany's interest was limited to ensuring that a situation did not arise in which Russia could threaten her penetration and control of Turkey, and she would only act if Austria-Hungary required her backing. Grey was able to get the consent of all the Powers to setting up a conference in London that consisted of their respective ambassadors with Grey in the chair.

The conference worked smoothly in a calm, amicable atmosphere. It held its first meeting in December 1912 and had persuaded the belligerents to sign a treaty of peace, the Treaty of London, by the end of May 1913. Unfortunately the terms of the treaty so far dissatisfied Bulgaria that her ruler, Prince Ferdinand, fell on Serbia without warning at the end of June. War broke out again, and Greece, Turkey and Romania all attacked Bulgaria. By the end of July she was hopelessly beaten and had to sue for peace. A peace conference opened in Bucharest on 31 July and the Treaty of Bucharest was signed on 10 August 1913. Bulgaria had to cede territory to Serbia, Greece and Romania. She hoped that the London Conference, which was still technically in session, would intervene to revise the terms, but in vain. Neither Russia nor Germany was ready for this. The conference took no action.

These events had transformed the Balkan situation: Turkey had almost vanished from Europe; the Balkan peoples had converted themselves into independent, national states, as Gladstone had envisaged, and there was some reason to hope that they would form a resilient buffer between Austria-Hungary and Russia; Serbia was resentful of the creation of Albania and more proudly patriotic than ever; Bulgaria was embittered; Romania, encouraged by its gains from Bulgaria, looked with sharper eyes across the Carpathians at Transylvania, which was largely inhabited by Romanians. Material for future strife there was. But the harmonious co-operation of the ambassadors and the success of the conference in handling the Balkan problem had renewed confidence and relaxed tension among the Great Powers. In this calmer atmosphere the news of the murder of Archduke Francis Ferdinand, heir to the Habsburg Empire, by a Bosnian Serb at Sarajevo on 28 June 1914 produced shock and indignation but no great alarm.

For a month after the murder at Sarajevo nothing happened. Life went on as usual, and people looked forward to their summer holidays. On 23 July Lloyd George told the House of Commons that Britain's relations with Germany were better than they had been for years. On the same day Austria-Hungary sent an ultimatum to Serbia implying Serbian complicity in the Archduke's murder, demanding that the Austrian government should collaborate with the Serbian government *in* Serbia to bring those responsible for the murder to justice, and setting a time limit of forty-eight hours for an answer. Grey described the ultimatum as 'the most formidable document that I have ever seen addressed by one State to another that was independent'. To everyone's surprise Serbia returned a mild answer on 25 July accepting practically all the points of the ultimatum and even agreeing to Austrian collaboration on Serbian soil subject to the principles of international law. Grey, who, so long as the Austrian government had made no open move, had limited himself to taking steps to localise a war between Austria-Hungary and Serbia, should it break out, immediately proposed the revival of the London Conference to deal with the situation. It was an idle move, for Austria-Hungary had already decided on war with Serbia, and unknown to the other Powers had on 5 July secured 'a blank cheque' from Germany to take what action she considered appropriate. On 28 July she declared war on Serbia, and Germany turned down Grey's proposal for a conference. On the 30th Russia ordered mobilisation. On the same day the chief of the German general staff, Moltke, before hearing of the Russian mobilisation order, recommended Austria-Hungary to mobilise and announced that Germany too would mobilise. On the 31st Germany sent an ultimatum to Russia and on 1 August declared war. At the same time Germany demanded a promise of neutrality from France. France refused, the French prime minister answering, 'France will act in accordance with her interests.' Germany, whose military plan entailed an attack first on France, accordingly declared war on 3 August.

What would Britain do? She was not committed to fight for either France or Russia. But diplomatic relations and military and naval conversations had drawn Britain and France steadily closer. Grey always denied, at the time and afterwards, that there was any moral obligation to come to the help of France. He stuck to his policy to the end. He warned Germany not to count on British neutrality; he warned France and Russia not to count on British support. Others were not so sure. Morley, an out-and-out critic of Grey's policy, contended that it had committed the country to France. Nicolson shared his opinion: through the military conversations 'the government had committed itself to a guarantee which would involve England either in a breach of faith or a war with Germany'. Paul Cambon said to Wickham Steed, Foreign Editor of *The Times*, while the government was making up its mind, 'I am waiting to know if the word honour should be erased from the English language.'

Honour apart, what Grey feared, as he had feared all along, was a split in the Cabinet, in Parliament and in the country. He did not believe that a war between Germany and France, even a war declared by Germany, would inevitably seem to most of his fellow-countrymen a threat to British interests or an insult to British honour. This was no timid or frivolous belief: as it was, Morley and Burns resigned from the Cabinet rather than be parties to the war. But German action saved Grey from his dilemma. On 3 August Germany sent an ultimatum to Belgium demanding free passage for her troops to invade France. The Belgian government rejected the ultimatum. Grey rose to speak to a crowded House of Commons just before 3 o'clock on Bank Holiday Monday, 3 August. He looked gaunt and haggard from intense work and strain. 'His face was passionless,' noted an observer, quoted by Keith Robbins in his biography of Grey, 'and sharply cut like a bird's, his voice was clear, with no warm tones in it, his language was wholly unadorned, precise, simple, accurate, austerely dignified.' He devoted the first part of his speech to a review of Great Britain's relations with France, stressing that the country was not committed to her defence and had complete freedom of action, but adding, 'how far [friendship with France] entails an obligation let every man look into his own heart, and his own feelings, and construe the extent of the obligation for himself. I construe it myself as I feel it.' He then turned to Belgium and gave the House an account of Britain's treaty obligations to her. He read King Albert's appeal to King George V received that morning. He added: 'If Belgium's independence goes, the independence of Holland will follow. I ask the House, from the point of view of British interests, to consider what is at stake. If France is beaten in a struggle of life and death ... becomes subordinate to the will and power of one greater than herself ... I do not believe, for a moment, that at the end of this war, even if we stood aside and remained aside, we should be in a position, a material position, to use our force decisively to undo what had happened in the course of the war, to prevent the whole of Western Europe opposite to us—if that had been the result of the war—falling under the domination of a single power, and I am quite sure that our moral position would be such as to have lost us all respect.' Grey carried the House with him. There was a corresponding swing of opinion in the country. On 4 August the Cabinet authorised Grey to send an ultimatum to Germany, protesting against the violation of Belgian neutrality and requiring a satisfactory reply by midnight. 'Grey, Asquith and others', writes Keith Robbins, 'sat around in the Cabinet room, smoking and waiting. There was no reply.'

Grey's policy has, naturally, been much criticised. A favourite German line at the time and after the war was that Grey was the agent of a policy of encirclement—even so fine a historian as Franz Schnabel accuses England of making deliberate sacrifices of her interests to France and Russia in order 'to complete the isolation of Germany'. The absurdity of this accusation on psychological grounds is apparent to anyone who has read anything about Grey; but it can be refuted on purely factual grounds, for the documents show that Grey encouraged efforts to reach agreement with Turkey and Germany on the Baghdad railway and to satisfy what he regarded as her legitimate ambitions in Asia Minor. It can only be made plausible by arguing that he was in the hands of his officials at the Foreign Office, who were bent on a policy of isolation. But the plausibility of this argument has been undermined by Mrs. Steiner, who shows conclusively that Grey was by no means a cypher in the hands of his officials and, further, that there was considerable difference of opinion among the most important of them about the policy to be followed towards Germany.

More serious are criticisms made at the time by some of Grey's colleagues in Parliament and in the Foreign Office and subsequently echoed by a number of historians by no means unsympathetic to British policy. It is argued on the one hand that Grey's policy was too indefinite: if only he had converted the ententes into alliances Germany would have known for certain that Britain was an enemy and would have been deterred from going to war. The short answer to this is that it was impossible, or at least impossible for a Liberal government. Liberals in Parliament and in the country were divided about the Entente and would not have tolerated its being turned into an alliance. Whether a Conservative government could have converted the country to such a policy is a matter for speculation; it is almost wholly idle in view of the hectic atmosphere generated by the controversy over the House of Lords and Home Rule for Ireland. Furthermore, even if he could have converted the Entente into an alliance Grey would not have done so. 'He had not sufficient confidence', as G. M. Trevelyan writes, 'that the pacific intentions of France and Russia would survive the positive assurance of British support in every possible case.' Grey himself put the point to the House of Commons in these words: 'Our friendship with France and Russia is in itself a guarantee that neither of them will pursue a provocative or aggressive policy to Germany. Any support we would give France or Russia in time of trouble would depend entirely on the feeling of Parliament and public feeling here when the trouble came, and both France and Russia know perfectly well that British opinion would not give support to provocative or aggressive action against Germany.' Nor is it by any means certain that an alliance, rather than an entente, would have deterred Germany, for there was a division of opinion towards Britain between the Kaiser and his civilian advisers on the one hand and the general staff on the other. Whatever view the critics take, the fact remains that Germany did not respect Belgian neutrality but invaded Belgium; this is what brought Britain into the war.

Other critics, of whom Loreburn and Morley are two of the earliest and best, argue that Grey had committed Britain too much to France and Russia. Had there been no military conversations Britain would, in fact as well as form, have had a free hand. This might not have prevented the war breaking out, but it would have meant that the country had the opportunity to decide if it would fight or not. Here again the crucial question is Belgium. In August 1914 hardly anyone in the country knew of the military conversations; it would have made virtually no difference to their feelings and thoughts if there had in fact been no conversations. In their ignorance they felt that the invasion of Belgium was not to be tolerated. Belgium was invaded and they felt they must fight.

Some critics have developed this line of argument into an allegation that Grey sacrificed British to French interests. It is undeniable that if Britain had not entered the war it would have saved millions of lives, millions of pounds and the psychological exhaustion that resulted from four years of trench warfare. Undeniably British troops fought in the first instance for French soil; undeniably British ships protected the Atlantic coast of France from German attack; undeniably France played a dominant part in settling the terms of the Versailles Treaty, with its consequences for the later history of Europe. But there are two insistent questions to be put: would Germany have defeated France and Russia but for British help? If Germany had won would she have established a hegemony of Europe with Britain either as a humble client or as a beaten foe? Neither question can be answered with certainty, but the consensus of expert opinion is that Germany would have won. The second question remains: the answer to it turns again on a judgment of German policy. This is to be found at the end of the next chapter.

Chapter V

The causes of the First World War

1 Economic causes During and immediately after the war an explanation of the causes of the war in economic terms was very popular, as in H. N. Brailsford, *The War of Steel and Gold* (1917) or Leonard Woolf, *Empire and Commerce in Africa* (1920). These derive from J. A. Hobson's celebrated book *Imperialism* (1902) and Lenin's *Imperialism: The Highest Stage of Capitalism* (1917), and ultimately from Marx. Both Hobson and Lenin fixed on the export of capital as the distinguishing mark of imperialism. Imperialism, in Lenin's definition, was the highest stage of capitalism, i.e. monopoly capitalism. What had happened was that through cartels, trusts and holding companies the banks and big industrialists had combined to monopolise capital. The search to invest this capital as profitably as possible led them to overseas markets; they could not invest it at home in agriculture and so raise the standard of living of the people, for this would contradict the basic motive of capitalism, to maximise profits. It must increase its profits, and this involves the export of capital to backward countries where 'profits are unusually high, for capital is scarce, the price of land is relatively low, wages are low, raw materials are cheap'. The export of capital had led to the complete territorial division of the world among the greatest capitalist Powers and in 1914 to war between them for world dominance.

There is no doubt that the great Powers did invest large sums overseas; Britain alone invested as much as £3,500 million between 1870 and 1914. It is a fact that the governments of

France, Germany and Russia kept a tight control over their money markets and used loans for definite political purposes. It is a fact that in certain areas of the world such as China and Persia, the governments, including the British government, or syndicates backed by the governments, competed in making loans designed to give them political leverage or to counter the efforts of rival Powers. But the Lenin thesis is open to several objections. In the first place cartels and trusts played a major part in the economic life of Germany and the U.S.A., but a much smaller one in France and Britain; yet neither France nor Britain was backward in the scramble for colonial territory. Furthermore, in Germany and the U.S.A. the formation of cartels came after the high point of imperialism had been passed, often after 1900, so it can hardly serve as a cause. Detailed investigation of interest rates has cast doubt on the thesis that overseas interest rates were in the nature of things higher than home rates; rates for highly speculative ventures were higher. Great profits were made from, for example, diamonds and gold. But many colonial companies, like the British East Africa Company, never made a profit. Lastly, by no means all overseas investment went into colonial territories: almost 70 per cent of British investment between 1870 and 1914 went to the U.S.A., Canada, Argentina, S. Africa and Australia: of these the only countries that could be regarded as colonial areas in Lenin's sense were Argentina and S. Africa, who took between them about a quarter of the whole amount.

In discussing the division of the world by the great Powers between about 1880 and 1900 Lenin also suggested that they needed to expand to gain raw materials and markets, and to export population. Clearly they needed certain raw materials that they did not possess at home, such as oil from Persia, vegetable oil from W. Africa, and rubber from S. America. Yet they divided out the world without much regard to these: Persia, as we have seen, on purely strategic lines; W. Africa by a process of grab and haggle; S. America not at all. On the other hand the lure of potential raw materials may have been important. German S.W. Africa was a desert, but it might contain gold and diamonds to the same extent as Transvaal.

As markets the colonial territories were disappointing. Wages were low, as Lenin remarked; but this cuts two ways. The worker is cheap, but he has little purchasing power. He cannot buy much and he may not want what the exporter has to offer. A hungry man would as soon have a stone as a ball-bearing; a thirsty man rather a gourd of palm-wine than a bottle of sulphuric acid. Nevertheless the African colonies were a market for cheap cottons from Manchester and to a lesser extent for hardware from Birmingham. It seems also to be true that merchants had greater expectations of the markets than they fulfilled. They formed colonial lobbies in France, Germany and Britain: in Marseilles, Hamburg, Manchester, Liverpool, Glasgow and Birmingham.

Only for Germany and Italy did emigration play any considerable part as a motive for colonial expansion. Millions of Germans and Italians emigrated to the U.S.A. Restrictions on immigration were discussed in American political circles for twenty years before the war but were only enacted by Congress in 1917. By contrast there were by 1911 less than 10,000 Germans living in German colonies, 1500 of them soldiers or officials, as compared with 150,000 German colonists on Polish soil. Thousands of Italians went across the straits to Tunis, but it was France, not Italy, that annexed Tunisia. After 1881 Italians went to Libya and Tripolitania, and in 1912 Italy took them from Turkey. Emigration may have been necessary for Germans and Italians from an economic point of view. It clearly did not constitute an economic cause of war. On the other hand many Germans and Italians were distressed at the idea of so many of their fellow-countrymen emigrating to America and being lost to their fatherlands, becoming instead citizens of the U.S.A. or Argentina or Brazil. They ardently longed for their brothers to settle in colonies of their own and to extend the bounds of *Deutschtum* or *Italia*. An analogous idea lay behind the French policy of assimilation: the citizen of Dakar differs from the Parisian only in the colour of his skin: a Frenchman is a Frenchman is a Frenchman.

Whatever the importance of these economic conflicts it remains true that the division of the world did not lead to international war. The frontiers of Africa were largely settled by 1900; the spheres of influence in China, Tibet, Afghanistan, S.E. Asia and Persia by 1907. The only considerable war that arose out of these conflicts was the Russo-Japanese War, and this led to the co-operation of the two Powers in the exploitation of Manchuria and Korea.

2 Biological and psychological causes About the turn of the century what has been called 'Social Darwinism' was much in vogue. Starting from Darwin's hypothesis that natural selection was the mechanism for the evolution of the species, publicists crudely distorted the notion of species adapting to their environment into that of 'the survival of the fittest'. The fittest were those who conquered their environment by force: Nature was red in tooth and claw because blood was the symbol of evolutionary progress! They then went on to apply this dogma by analogy to nations or states conceived as organisms. A few quotations will give an idea of their thought.

'Force is the decisive factor in the world; nations maintain themselves by strength of combat and unity of purpose and not by superiority of civilisation.' (Karl Benedikt Haase) 'We must play a great part in the world, and especially . . . perform those deeds of blood, of valour, which above everything else bring national renown.' (Theodore Roosevelt) 'Storm purifies the air and destroys the frail trees, leaving the sturdy oaks standing. War is the test of a nation's political, physical, and intellectual worth. The State in which there is much that is rotten may vegetate for a while in peace, but in war its weakness is revealed.' (Karl von Stengel, a jurist who was one of Germany's delegates to the first Hague Peace Conference.) 'War is one of the conditions of progress, the sting which prevents a country from going to sleep, and compels satisfied mediocrity itself to awaken from its apathy.' (Ernest Renan.) 'War is one of the elements of order in the world established by God. The noblest virtues of men are developed therein. Without war the world would degenerate and disappear in a morass of materialism.' (Moltke.) There is a trace of this attitude even in Sir Edward Grey, who 'would go out of his way to avoid a company of Kitchener's recruits marching down a cheering street': 'If we fall into a position of inferiority our self-respect is gone, and it removes that enterprise which is essential both to the material success of industry and to the carrying out of ideals, and you fall into a state of apathy.' The writings of publicists are not of course infallible evidence of how people behave, nor do they inevitably make them behave according to their dogmas, though they may well influence their behaviour. But the psychologists from their own angle produced much supporting evidence.

The human mind, its functions and processes, had been studied for centuries by philosophers, but it was only at this time that the work of experimental psychologists transferred its study from the domain of philosophy to that of science. They devoted much time and attention to the instincts. William McDougall listed as many as sixteen, of which aggression and self-assertion were two. Alfred Adler, who came to the conclusion that a sense of inferiority or inadequacy was the root of human conduct, accepted aggression as a symptom of this feeling and defined it as any manifestation of what he called 'the will-to-power'. Sigmund Freud, who insisted that an instinct must not be reducible to simpler components, in his later work postulated two instincts only: a love or life instinct that he called Eros, and a death instinct that he called Thanatos. He defined aggression as any manifestation in conscious behaviour of the death instinct. Furthermore, Freud in his psycho-analytical work developed the notion of the subconscious and the connection of the instincts with it. The work of the psychologists had placed instinct in a new context and altered the whole concept of personality. It had also produced a mass of evidence to show that aggressiveness is a common human trait 'under specified environmental conditions and specified drive conditions'.

But this is not the end of it. It is obvious that behaviour may be very different in a member of a group from what it is in an individual. It is enough to think of fashions in clothes or crazes that mysteriously spread through a school or other society to be aware of this. Collective behaviour may however take forms nearer to our purpose. Panic may seize a theatre audience if fire breaks out and cause people to rush the doors regardless of the danger of being crushed to death. Stranger and more akin to war hysteria is the well-authenticated reaction of the listeners to a radio programme, *The Invasion from Mars*, on 30 October 1938: hundreds rang up to discover if the rumour were true, many took to the cellar or to the roads in panic flight. Mass hysteria can take hold of a crowd and cause it to riot for hours on end. Mass hysteria plus something else can produce a lynching. No one man can lynch another; a crowd can and does.

An emotion of this sort may show itself collectively as a desire to humiliate another nation, as the French perhaps showed on the eve of the Franco-Prussian war, or even as a desire for war itself. It has been suggested that after the lapse of a generation a nation is subconsciously bored with peace and anxious for war. This theory can hardly yet be tested against sufficient experience, as nations have been in existence for too short a time. But it is possible to set certain pieces of evidence against each other. By 1895 a generation had elapsed since the Franco-Prussian war of 1870; neither France nor Germany had been at war in the intervening twenty-five years. Austria-Hungary had not been at war since 1866 (but the internal ethnic tensions must not be forgotten). Except for the Venetian campaign of 1866 Italy had not been at war since the creation of the kingdom in 1860. Russia had been heavily involved with the Japanese in 1904 and had suffered a shattering defeat. Britain had not been involved in a continental war since the Crimean War, but the S. African War, though a colonial war, had turned out much tougher than anyone had expected and had had a damaging effect on the nation's morale.

Whatever may be thought of this theory there is overwhelming evidence that the war was welcomed in 1914 in all European countries. 'There was jubilation in Europe in the early days of August 1914', writes Golo Mann, 'as well as aggressive fury and aggressive enthusiasm. . . . It would be wrong to say that at this moment [the peoples of Europe] in their heart of hearts wanted to preserve the peace. The war would be short and glorious, an exciting, liberating adventure. God would be on everybody's side and everybody would win.' It is easy to illustrate his generalisation.

On 28 July a young American wrote to his mother from Dresden. 'Last night the streets were filled by masses of people singing patriotic songs until two o'clock in the morning and shouting "Long live Austria", which had just declared war on Serbia. . . . The threat of war . . . drives the whole world mad. I became very thoughtful when I heard masses of young people march through the streets long past midnight singing *Die Wacht am Rhein*. Their activities will give the statesmen . . . a good excuse for their own folly, because they can say they were forced into it by the enthusiasm of the masses.' (Quoted by Golo Mann in *The History of Germany since 1789*, Chatto and Windus, 1968, p. 303.) In St. Petersburg huge crowds gathered in front of the Winter Palace, knelt to sing the national anthem and then surged off to sack the German embassy.

On the night of 4 August in London 'a vast, excited concourse had gathered in the Mall surrounding Buckingham Palace, and spreading far across the Green Park. Their cheering swelled into a Niagaran roar as the King and Queen, with the Prince of Wales, appeared on the balcony. Then someone struck up "God Save the King" and 30,000 people sang. Farther up the Mall, by the Duke of York's Steps, another patriotic section were smashing the windows of the German Embassy, and the mounted police had to be fetched from Cannon Row.' (Frank Owen, *Tempestuous Journey*, Hutchinson, 1954, p. 270.)

3 Military causes Modern war however is not a matter of spontaneous combustion, but of careful planning and preparation. It involves great masses of men and material. In 1914 mobilisation required not hours but days; Russia could not undertake to have 800,000 men ready to attack East Prussia before the eighteenth day of mobilisation. A dreadnought took a year to build. Modern war also involves large sums of money. The defence estimates of the belligerent Powers increased by over two-and-a-half times between 1890 and 1914.

Germany, Britain and Russia spent the most. Germany and Britain could afford to; Russia could do so if she could tap her unused resources and develop an efficient financial system.

Defence estimates of the Great Powers 1890–1914
(in millions of £s)

	1890	1900	1910	1914
Germany	28·8	41	64	110·8
Austria	12·8	13·6	17·4	36·4
France	37·4	42·4	52·4	57·4
Britain	31·4	116	68	76·8
Russia	29	40·8	63·4	88·2

(The British figure for 1900 is due to the cost of the South African War)
Figures from A. J. P. Taylor.

It has been argued that an arms race leads inevitably to war. It is true that arms manufacturers like other manufacturers want to sell their wares. But arms are not quite like bicycles or cotton shirts. A bicycle is more or less indestructible and a cotton shirt is normally worn, once bought, till it is worn out. The bicycle manufacturer to make a profit must extend his market; the cotton manufacturer expects his shirt to be in the end consumed and he may then hope to sell a replacement. The arms manufacturer is in a different position. His goods are not indestructible nor necessarily consumed. Arms become obsolete, in modern conditions rapidly obsolete; he may look to replace arms continuously and fairly quickly. He does not need a war to make a profit. It is however true that he will sell much more in a war, especially in a long and hard-fought war. If he is determined to maximise his profits, he may calculate that a war will be good for business; but it should not be forgotten that a good business man will look to the more distant future as well as to the present and immediately after. Nor is the business man purely economic man; he is a human being and a citizen—that is unless the Marxist argument is accepted, that a capitalist is compelled by the logic of the capitalist system to maximise profits; in which case, unless there were a continuously expanding arms market outside the Great Power market, the arms manufacturer would be compelled, whatever his personal inclinations, to work for war. But war would still not be inevitable.

It has been argued that it is inevitable on two different grounds: by the Marxists and by a school of thought of which Lowes

Dickinson may be taken as representative. The Marxist argument is simply an extension of the argument that the capitalist is compelled to behave as he does by the capitalist system. So too is the politician. For politics are a mere consequence of economics. Politicians may believe they are in control of their actions and are carrying out policies they have conceived and formulated, but this is an illusion. They are not their own masters, but the capitalists' servants. Their function is to use the state apparatus in accordance with the laws of capitalist development. As capitalism develops into imperialism and imperialism into war, foreign policy and armaments policy match this development. The arms manufacturers, obeying the law of their being, strive to maximise profits; the arms race gathers momentum. The politicians are helpless to control it. At some point, inevitably the guns go off.

Lowes Dickinson wrote in the preface to *The International Anarchy* (Allen and Unwin, 1926) 'My thesis is, that whenever and wherever the anarchy of armed States exists, war does become inevitable.' He goes on to describe the anarchy of armed states between 1870 and 1914. That there were states in Europe during that time is self-evident; that they were armed is demonstrated by the figures; that there was anarchy in the sense that the states were sovereign, owing allegiance to no higher authority, is true. But it is also true that there were armed states in Europe between 1815 and 1854, when there were no European wars, though they were, admittedly, less heavily armed than at the end of the century. This raises the question whether it is the sovereignty or the armaments of the states that inevitably produces war, or some indeterminate but essential mixture of the two—which comes first, the hen or the egg, or are they twin ingredients of one omelette? It seems, however, at least doubtful whether wars arise simply because sovereign states have come into existence. Each state as a sovereign body is independent and fully in control of its own internal life. But it is surrounded by other sovereign states. Their policies may clash. But the form of the clash is not laid down in advance; it depends on their military and political plans.

The war plans of all the belligerents except Britain called for an initial offensive; military orthodoxy held that it was vital to seize and hold the initiative. This was despite much military experience: despite the demonstrated power of the French *chassepots* at Gravelotte and of the Remingtons used by the Turks at Plevna; despite the way in which the Russians had been held up at Plevna and the Bulgars by the Chatalja lines; despite 'the reinforcement brought to the defensive', as Sir Denis Brogan suggests in *The Development of Modern France* (Hamish Hamilton, 1967, p. 468) 'by the improvements in equipment, the magazine rifle, the effective machine-gun, the quick-firing field-gun and smokeless powder'. This was true of Russia, even after her disastrous defeat by Japan and even though she was in process of reorganising her forces and constructing a network of strategic railways in Poland that could not be ready before 1916. It was true of France, although her population in 1910 was only 39 million to Germany's 65 million, and she had spent millions of francs in fortifying the French frontier from Verdun in the north to the Swiss frontier. Despite this situation France in 1913 adopted a new war plan, Plan 17, that called for an offensive in Lorraine aimed at the supposed centre of the German line, and introduced three years' military service instead of two, so as to make up in part for the German superiority in numbers.

The war plans corresponded to the spirit and strength of the war parties on the Continent. In Austria the chief of the imperial staff, Conrad von Hötzendorf, presented to the Emperor an annual proposal for war, either against Italy or against Serbia. For his interference in foreign affairs he was dismissed from his post in November 1911 but re-appointed in December 1912. In Russia there was a continual battle for control over the Tsar; in 1904 the war party had pushed Russia into war; in the years after 1905 the impact of defeat and revolution had had a sobering effect. But gradually the Russians recovered their self-confidence, and, with it, their appetite for war. In Germany the Prussian tradition of government was deep-rooted. William II, despite his physique and temperament, regarded himself as having a natural affinity with the armed forces, especially with the navy, and successive German chancellors failed to assert the authority of the civilian government and the Reichstag over the service chiefs.

Of great importance too in relation to the outbreak of the First World War was the German war plan. While the plans of all the European states called for an offensive, the German plan was the only one that was based on the assumption of a war on two fronts. The Schlieffen Plan, it will be remembered, aimed at delivering a knock-out blow to France before turning to engage Russia. Whereas each of the other Powers could if it wished fight a localised war, Austria-Hungary, for example, against Serbia, Russia against China, or even perhaps Turkey, France against Germany, Germany could not, unless she first abandoned the Schlieffen Plan and recast her military policy.

4 Political causes The war plans of the Powers reflected their political nature. The Powers had interests which were assumed to be permanently and mutually incompatible. From this situation emerged a certain balance of power, which, at any given time, was more or less stable, and, consequently, more or less favourable to peace. Between 1815 and 1870 it had been pretty stable, partly because of the defeat of Napoleon's bid for European hegemony and partly, perhaps, as E. H. Carr argues in *Nationalism and After*, because the nationalism of the Powers was contained in a strong, though largely invisible, international structure, centred on London and based on British naval and economic strength. After 1870 the balance of power became more and more unstable, as British strength weakened and Germany emerged more and more clearly as the strongest Power in Europe. But the balance was precarious not only in this straightforward sense. Some of the Powers were themselves unstable and there were certain areas of the world that were specially unstable.

The most obviously unstable of the Powers was Austria-Hungary. The Habsburg Empire had come near to disintegration in 1848. Since then the force of nationalism had got stronger, not weaker. The Slavs were a headache for all Austrian politicians, and Franz Ferdinand's action in attending the army manoeuvres in Bosnia in June 1914 was regarded as so provocative that the authorities did their best to stop his going; his action in fact proved suicidal. At bottom there was a fundamental disequilibrium between economic and political power: economic power lay with the landowners and business men whose fortunes depended on the large, unified Danube market; political power was in the hands of the Hungarians, who vetoed any attempt to solve the problem of the nationalities. With the continuing development of national self-consciousness this could only mean in the end some sort of explosion.

Russia's lack of stability was equally serious but less obvious. It is now clear that tsardom very nearly collapsed in 1905. It was clear even then to the Russian minister Stolypin, whose land policy was designed to remove the basic cause of revolution and to bring into being a class of peasant owners who would have been as stable a support for the tsarist regime as the peasant proprietors of France were to the Napoleonic Empire, and, later, to the Third Republic. There was not enough time before war broke out in 1914 for his policy to prove itself. But this is no matter for the present purpose. Contemporary European statesmen were ignorant alike of the problem and of Stolypin's attempted solution. They all overrated Russian power.

Germany was not unstable in the way Austria-Hungary and Russia were. She had indeed minorities, Alsatian, Danish and Polish, but in the main the population was homogeneous, loyal and intelligent, and industrious beyond the normal. She had no depressed class corresponding to the Russian peasantry. Bismarck's failure to crush the Roman Catholics and the Socialists had left the country stronger rather than weaker. Nevertheless all was not well. The structure of the state was unsound, as has been shown by German historians, among them Fritz Fischer and Golo Mann. What Bismarck had designed as a sham to deny real political power to the people and to deceive them into thinking they had it, through the Reichstag, did not deceive everyone and did not stand up to the strains put on it by the war. As early as 1904 Jaurès had said: 'Even if you [German Socialists] got a majority in the Reichstag, you are the only country in which a Socialist majority in Parliament would not mean a Socialist mastery over the country. For your Parliament is but a half-Parliament, without executive power, without governmental power; its decisions are merely advisory, and the imperial authorities may reverse them at their will.' This was nothing but the truth. The Kaiser and the armed forces ruled the roost. But in defeat the Kaiser had to abdicate, the German empire came to an end, the navy vanished, the army temporarily took cover and a new constitution was worked out for the Weimar Republic.

It is not difficult to see the areas of maximum instability in the world at the turn of the century—North Africa, the Balkans, Persia and China. By 1911 two of these had ceased to trouble the Powers. As a result of the Agadir crisis France was confirmed as the paramount Power in Morocco as well as in Algeria and Tunisia, and Britain in Egypt. China was in a state of chaos and revolution, an invitation to the Powers to intervene, but Russia and Japan had come to an understanding which for the time being held firm and prevented a further scramble for China. Persia was still the scene of conflict between Russia and Britain, and, as we have seen, Grey recorded that 'Persia tried my patience more than any other subject'. But there was little risk of war. Russia held too many cards: Persia was too far away from England to be a convenient theatre of war; neither the British nor the Indian Army was strong enough to take on the Russians, nor could they have been enlarged, even by conscription, to do so; and the British Navy, as Rouvier remarked, 'could not run on wheels'.

There remained the Balkans. As long ago as 1815 Metternich's adviser Gentz had written: 'The end of the Turkish monarchy could be survived by the Austrian for but a short time.' The great French historian Albert Sorel expressed the same idea more vividly: 'As soon as Turkey has left the sick man's bed Austria will get into it.' In 1914 Turkey was still in the bed, but the Sultan was near his end, and the frontier of Turkey-in-Europe ran not much more than a hundred miles from Constantinople. Two questions clamoured for an answer. What was to happen in the Balkans? What was to happen to Constantinople?

Since Gentz's day national feeling had become immensely stronger and much more self-conscious. The Balkan Wars had shown not only its strength but its effectiveness and its boomerang quality. The Balkan League had driven the Turks almost out of

Europe, but its members had then fallen out and fought each other. The victors, Serbia and Greece, together with Romania, had then imposed new frontiers on Bulgaria by the Treaty of Bucharest. Bulgaria was embittered and nursed her revenge. More serious, victorious and pugnacious Serbia was frustrated: frustrated by failure to gain access to the Adriatic and by the creation of what she regarded as the bogus state of Albania, and frustrated by her knowledge that several million Serbs lived within the borders of the Habsburg Empire. It was not likely that the Balkan frontiers would remain long unchanged. But it was uncertain who would first attempt to change them.

In the event it was Austria-Hungary. There is no doubt about the immediate cause of the war that began in August 1914. It was Austria-Hungary's action in sending the ultimatum to Serbia on 23 July and declaring war on 28 July. She had decided to solve the Serbian question by force, by destroying the kingdom of Serbia and incorporating its inhabitants in the Habsburg Empire. But this meant war only between Austria and Serbia. Why did this in a week develop into the First World War?

First, the Balkan question was interwoven with the question of Constantinople. In 1908 by the Buchlau agreement Austria-Hungary and Russia were to act together in their own interests: Austria-Hungary by annexing Bosnia, Russia by gaining control of the Straits and Constantinople. But Austria-Hungary acted alone in 1908 and left Russia high and dry. Izvolsky was livid, and determined to get his revenge sooner or later. This might not have been of much consequence if it had merely been Izvolsky's private feeling, particularly after he ceased to be foreign minister in 1910, but Russia shared his feeling. She felt she could not endure another such humiliating diplomatic defeat. This was partly because of the blow to her prestige, partly because of its effect on the Slavs in the Balkans, who looked to Russia as their fellow-Slav protector against Austria-Hungary. Russian diplomacy in Belgrade and Sofia was a sign of this feeling. The results of this diplomacy were gratifying, but they stopped short of clearing the Turks right out of Europe and occupying Constantinople in their stead.

Secondly, Russia could not afford to let down Serbia. Russian diplomacy had promoted the first Balkan War and had given full backing to the Balkan Slavs against Turkey. But Russia had also co-operated in the ambassadors' conference in London to prevent a European war arising out of the Balkan War, and in so doing had lost some of her lustre in Serbian eyes. If she failed to support Serbia when directly attacked by Austria-Hungary she feared that she would lose all influence with the Serbs and throughout the Balkans; she would be revealed as having not only feet of clay but a heart of jelly.

Thirdly, Austria-Hungary and Russia did not stand alone. Each was a member of a power-bloc: Austria-Hungary of the Triple Alliance, Russia of the Triple Entente. Originally the Austro-German Alliance of 1879 and the Franco-Russian Alliance of 1894 had been strictly defensive. But in the twentieth century both had been altered. In 1909 Moltke, with the approval of the Kaiser and Bülow, wrote to his Austrian opposite number Conrad in answer to a letter from him asking what would be the German attitude in the event of Russia's going to war with Austria as a result of an Austrian attack on Serbia. Part of his letter reads as follows: 'It is to be foreseen that the time will come when the longanimity of the Monarchy in face of Serb provocation will come to an end. Then nothing will remain but for her to enter Serbia.

'I think that only an Austrian invasion of Serbia by Austria could, in the event, lead to active intervention by Russia. This would provide the *casus foederis* for Germany. . . . The moment Russia mobilises, Germany also will mobilise, and will unquestionably mobilise her whole army.' This is without doubt a declaration that Germany would come in on Austria's side not only in the event of Austria's being attacked by Russia, as laid down in the 1879 alliance, but also in the event of a war occurring between Austria and Russia as a direct result of an Austrian attack on Serbia. Moltke and Conrad went on in further correspondence to agree on the military details: Germany would keep thirteen divisions in East Prussia and would attack France with the main body of its forces, while Austria-Hungary would take the offensive in Galicia.

The alteration of the Franco-Russian Alliance was not so clear-cut or so drastic, but seems nevertheless to be a fact. Originally France had been determined not to be dragged into a war in the Balkans, where she had no interests at stake. The alliance provided that France would help Russia if she were attacked 'by Germany or by Austria supported by Germany'. This showed clearly where French priorities lay and seemed safe enough, as it was highly unlikely that Austria-Hungary, even if assured of German backing, would herself initiate a war with Russia by attacking. But during 1912 French policy subtly changed. Instead of restraining Russia in the Balkans as before she appeared to be disappointed at Russia's mildness during the Balkan wars. In August 1912 Poincaré told Izvolsky, 'If conflict with Austria brought intervention by Germany, France would fulfil her obligations.' This is a formula in diplomatic language and its exact meaning is not beyond doubt, but it certainly goes further than the words of the original alliance.

Events in July 1914 followed expectation. Serb provocation, or apparent provocation, reached a climax in the murder of Archduke Franz Ferdinand. Austrian 'patience' was exhausted. On 28 July Austria-Hungary declared war on Serbia. On the same day Russia attempted to mobilise her forces against Austria-Hungary alone (a feat that proved beyond her technical competence). On 29 July the German government warned Russia that 'further continuation of Russian mobilisation would force us to mobilise also'. On 30 July Russia decreed general mobilisation. On 31 July Germany set German mobilisation in train. On 1 August she declared war on Russia; on 3 August on France. On the same day Germany sent her ultimatum to Belgium. Britain demanded its withdrawal. No answer. Accordingly Britain declared war on Germany on 4 August.

Responsibility for the outbreak of the war was endlessly debated in the period between the two world wars. The debate began with Article 231 of the Versailles Treaty, attributing sole responsibility to Germany and her allies—the 'War Guilt Clause'. It continued with the publication of selected documents in many volumes bearing on the problem: *Die grosse Politik der europäischen*

Kabinette, (40 vols, 1922–6); *Österreich-Ungarns Aussenpolitik*, (9 vols, 1930); *Documents diplomatiques français*, (32 vols, 1929–); *British Documents on the Origins of the War*, (11 vols, 1927–); *Mezhdunarodnye otnosheniya v epokhu imperializma*, (1930–). Many of the protagonists in the events leading up to the war and in the war itself contributed their memoirs: Bülow, Bethmann-Hollweg, Caillaux, Poincaré, Asquith, Grey, Lloyd George, Izvolsky, Sazonov. Historians got to work, laying the emphasis here or there. S. B. Fay laid the blame on all the Powers, beginning with Serbia for not doing all she could to prevent the Sarajevo murder and ending with France for egging Russia on instead of restraining her. Bernadotte Schmitt laid the blame principally on Germany. Alfred Wegerer spent years asserting Germany's complete innocence and putting the blame on the Entente. Pierre Renouvin thought that the Central Powers 'imposed war on the Triple *Entente*', while another French historian, Jules Isaac, countered by saying that 'the Triple *Entente* showed no great reluctance to meet the challenge'. But the consensus of opinion might be summed up in the words of the German historian Hermann Lutz: 'All the Powers in 1914 put their own interests, true or supposed, and their own ambitions before the peace of the world. . . . No belligerent except Belgium was blameless and none was the sole culprit.'

This consensus, which may be said to have been generally accepted by the middle of the twentieth century, has been challenged by the German historian Fritz Fischer in two huge books: *Griff nach der Weltmacht* (1961), translated into English under the title *Germany's Aims in the First World War* (1967), and *Krieg der Illusionen* (1969). Fischer's argument falls into four parts. First, the social and political structure of imperial Germany imposed a militaristic stamp on its politics. Secondly, a demagogic programme of annexation had developed in Germany before 1914 which aimed at creating three great spheres of influence, economic and political: *Mitteleuropa*, *Mittelafrika* and Asia Minor. Thirdly, Germany had begun to put this programme into practice before 1914, by pushing the Baghdad Railway, by the negotiations about the French Congo and the Portuguese colonies in Africa, and by building up the German fleet as an instrument of this policy. Finally, in the crisis of July 1914 the German government had determined on war from the beginning.

Fischer has been violently attacked by other German historians and with special viciousness by the late Gerhard Ritter. His attacks by their very viciousness lead one to feel that Fischer's argument cuts uncomfortably near the bone. On the other hand A. J. P. Taylor, who himself assigns the main responsibility for the war to Germany on other grounds, is not wholly convinced. He points out that, though German propagandists demanded the control of the iron-ore of Belgium and north-east France and the annexation of Russian Poland and the Ukraine to provide the Germans with enough food, German industrialists did not wait for their government to execute this policy but bought their way into the iron-ore concerns of north-east France and Normandy, while the German government, unable to provide all the capital itself, accepted it from British and French financiers to develop German trade with Asia Minor by means of the Baghdad railway. The German government undoubtedly built up the navy in the years before 1914, but 'the naval race with Great Britain . . . went on from its own momentum rather than from a deliberate pursuit of empire'.

What Fischer does seem to have demonstrated is that Germany was not dragged along in Austria-Hungary's wake. In July 1914 Austria-Hungary kicked over the traces and acted in a frivolous, irresponsible way, but Germany did nothing to restrain her, at least until it was too late. This means that in the last week before the war Grey's policy had no chance of success. Germany was not prepared to put pressure on Austria to stop the invasion of Serbia, and this deprived Grey of any means of influencing Russia.

In Fischer's interpretation Germany counted on British neutrality. This at least suggests the possibility that a definite Anglo-French alliance might have deterred Germany. But the evidence he has collected also makes this possibility remote. The alliance of the Junkers and the industrialists; the shrill nationalist appeal to the masses; the contempt for other peoples—the Russians barbarous, the French decadent, the English supine;

the weakness and instability of the Kaiser and his civilian advisers in contrast with the arrogant, but disciplined, self-confidence of the army and navy chiefs; at the end the abdication of the responsibility that inevitably falls on the shoulders of a great Power—these are the salient features that emerge from a close study of the landscape of the German Empire. Could any action of Britain's have deterred such a Germany?

Date Chart

1886   *Conservative government: Salisbury Prime Minister and* (January 1887) *Foreign Secretary*

1887   Mediterranean Agreements

1890   Fall of Bismarck. Colonial agreements with France, Germany and Portugal

1892   *Liberal government: Gladstone Prime Minister, Rosebery Foreign Secretary*

1894   *Rosebery Prime Minister, Kimberley Foreign Secretary.* Franco-Russian Alliance. British Protectorate over Uganda

1895   *Conservative government: Salisbury Prime Minister and Foreign Secretary*

1896   Kruger Telegram

1898   Fashoda. First German Navy Law

1899–1902   South African War

1900   Boxer Rebellion. *Salisbury resigns as Foreign Secretary* (October) *and is succeeded by Lansdowne*

1901   Death of Queen Victoria; accession of King Edward VII. Hay-Pauncefote Treaty

1902   Anglo-Japanese Alliance. *Salisbury resigns as Prime Minister and is succeeded by Balfour*

1903   Balfour reforms the Committee of Imperial Defence

1904   Entente Cordiale

1904–5   Russo-Japanese War

1905   Cawdor-Fisher naval reforms

1905   First Morocco Crisis. *Liberal government: Campbell-Bannerman Prime Minister, Grey Foreign Secretary*

1906   Algeciras Conference

1907   Anglo-Russian Entente. Haldane's army reforms

1908   *Campbell-Bannerman resigns and is succeeded by Asquith*

1909   Naval scare

1911   Second Morocco Crisis: Agadir

1912–13   Balkan Wars

1914   (June) Sarajevo. (August) First World War

Further Reading

Before grappling with British foreign policy the first essential is to get a firm grip on the international situation. For this purpose the best start is with Bernadotte E. Schmitt, *The Origins of the First World War* (Historical Association Pamphlet G.39, 1958) and Nicholas Mansergh, *The Coming of the First World War* (Longmans 1949). For fuller treatment Pierre Renouvin, *Histoire des Relations Internationales, Tome 6, Le XIX Siècle, II* (1955), particularly good on the economic background, and A. J. P. Taylor, *The Struggle for Mastery in Europe, 1848–1918* (O.U.P. 1954), an indispensable work of reference as well as vigorously arguing a point of view.

For British foreign policy there is no work covering the whole period; the most useful is Kenneth Bourne, *The Foreign Policy of Victorian England, 1850–1902* (O.U.P. 1970), a collection of documents with an extended and valuable introduction.

For the Foreign Office, Zara S. Steiner, *The Foreign Office and Foreign Policy, 1895–1914* (C.U.P. 1969).

For Salisbury, M. E. Chamberlain, *The New Imperialism* (Historical Association Pamphlet G.73, 1970); Lady Gwendolen Cecil, *Life of Robert, Marquis of Salisbury* (Hodder and Stoughton 5 vols. 1921–35), one of the finest biographies in English, though unfortunately stopping in 1892; J. A. S. Grenville, *Lord Salisbury and Foreign Policy* (Athlone Press 1964); R. Robinson and J. Gallagher, *Africa and the Victorians* (Macmillan 1961), a fascinating consideration of the role of Africa in British foreign policy; Lillian M. Penson, *Foreign Affairs under the Third Marquis of Salisbury* (Creighton Lecture in History, Athlone Press 1960).

For Rosebery, R. Rhodes James, *Rosebery* (Weidenfeld and Nicolson 1963); C. J. Lowe, *The Reluctant Imperialists* (Routledge and Kegan Paul 1967), two volumes, one of narrative and one of illustrative documents, covering the period down to 1902 and arranged by topics.

For Lansdowne, Grenville, *op. cit.*; G. S. Monger, *The End of Isolation* (Nelson 1963).

For Grey, Viscount Grey of Fallodon, *Twenty Five Years* (Hodder and Stoughton 1926), Grey's own narrative of his time as Foreign Secretary; Keith Robbins, *Sir Edward Grey* (Cassell 1971) and G. M. Trevelyan, *Grey of Fallodon* (Longmans 1937), two very well-written biographies.

For the navy, A. J. Marder, *British Naval Policy, 1860–1905* (Putnam 1940) and *From the Dreadnought to Scapa Flow, Volume 1, The Road to War, 1904–14* (O.U.P. 1961); and E. L. Woodward, *Great Britain and the German Navy* (O.U.P. 1935).

Index